EVERY SATURDAY IN AUTUMN

College Football's Greatest Traditions

by Ron Smith

PHOTO CREDITS

T = top, B = bottom, M = middle, R = right, L = left

Bob Leverone/TSN – CoverTL, 14, 17T, 26T, 27BL, 29TR, 78B, 80, 88B, 93, 102, 103, 104, 105, 106, 107, 108(2), 109, 110(2), 111, 148, 149B, 182, 185(2), 186(2), 187, 188(2), 189T, 190, 203, 204, 224.

Dilip Vishwanat/TSN – 612, 18, 20-21, 33, 34T, 41, 69B, 70, 153, 158T, 161(2), 176T.

Robert Seale/TSN – CoverTR, CoverR, 6TM, 35, 39T, 42, 43, 48TL, 211.

Paul Nisely/TSN – CoverBL, 47TL,

Albert Dickson/TSN – 24, 29BR, 66, 82, 91T, 92, 94, 95(2), 99, 100(2), 101B, 112, 113, 114, 115, 116TL, 117B, 119(2), 120, 121, 152, 156B, 158B, 205B, 206B, 212, 216T, 222.

TSN Archives – CoverT, 4-5, 13, 19, 38T, 40(2), 46(2), 47TR, 50B, 64, 65T, 67, 68, 69T, 74L, 75, 79T, 127, 141, 202, 208T, 209, 210B.

Peter Newcomb for TSN – 7BL, 15, 172, 173, 175, 176B, 177, 178, 179, 180, 181.

Ross Dettman for TSN – CoverB, 38B.

Sam Greenwood for TSN – 72, 81B.

John Cordes – 7BR, 17, 213, 214TL, 216B, 217T, 220(2), 221.

John Soohoo – 17B, 214BL, 215, 217B, 218-219.

Tony Tomsic – 98.

Stephen Morton for TSN – 134, 135, 136, 137(2), 138, 139(3), 140(2).

Todd Anderson for TSN – 210T.

Wil Moore/Ace Aerial Photography Inc. – OKC – 174.

Ken Ruinard/Anderson Independent Mail – 142, 144, 145(3), 149T.

Will Chandler/Anderson Independent Mail – 150.

Anderson Independent Mail – 7T, 143, 151.

Ryals Lee/Florida State University Photo – 206T, 207, 208B.

Susan Allen Sigmon/University of Texas Sports Photo – 192, 195, 196T, 197, 199B, 200B.

Jim Sigmon /University of Texas Sports Photo – Back Cover, 7B, 10, 193, 194(2), 196B, 198, 201.

Frank DiBrango – 7TR, 163, 164T, 165, 167B, 168, 169(2), 171.

Randy Hampton/Lincoln Journal Star – 6TR, 63.

Joe Raymond/Lincoln Journal Star – 32, 34B, 36, 37(3), 40T.

Eric Gregory/Lincoln Journal Star – 62.

William Lauer/Lincoln Journal Star – 71.

Robert Becker/Lincoln Journal Star – 67B.

Lincoln Journal Star – 65B.

Tom Raymond – 28TL.

Scott Halleran/Allsport – 28TR.

Mark Elias/AP/Wide World Photos – 39B.

Mark Wellman – 170.

University of Georgia – 7T, 133.

University of Tennessee – CoverM, 6TL, 22-23, 25, 26B, 27T, 27BR, 28B, 29BL.

Patrick Murphy-Racey – 10-11, 21TL, 29TL.

University of Washington – 184, 191.

United States Military Academy Admissions – 162, 164B, 166, 167T.

Paul Jaronski/University of Michigan Photo Services – 117T.

Bill Wood/University of Michigan Photo Services – 116B, 118.

Texas A&M University – 44, 48TR, 49, 50T.

Mississippi State University – 223.

Joanie Komura/University of Washington – 189B.

Brian Wagner for TSN – 30-31.

Jeff Miller/University of Wisconsin – Madison News & Public Affairs – 154, 155, 156T, 157, 159, 160.

Ray Carson/University of Florida – 6BL, 73, 74R, 76(2), 77(2).

Gene Bednarek/University of Florida – 79B.

Jeff Gage/University of Florida – 78T, 81T.

J. Rico Clement/LSU Sports Information – 56-57.

LSU Sports Archives – 55B

Steve Franz/LSU Sports Information – 6 – 7, 52, 53, 54, 55B, 55T, 58(2), 59(2), 60, 61.

Jay Crihfield for TSN – 117.

Jay Sailors for TSN – 7TL, 122, 123, 124, 125, 126(2), 128, 129, 130(2), 131.

Chris Carson/University of Texas Sports Photo – 199T, 200T.

Auburn University – 6BL, 83, 84, 85, 86, 87, 88T, 89, 90, 91B.

Clemson University – 146, 147.

Darren Carroll for TSN – 51.

David Gonzalez /University of Washington – 7BL, 183

Barth Falkenberg – 96(2), 97, 101T.

Bill Langford/Florida State University Photo – 205T.

Glen Johnson – 45, 47B.

Al Messerschmidt – 16, 132

The Sporting News is a federally registered trademark of Vulcan Sports Media, Inc. Visit our website at www.sportingnews.com.

ISBN: 0-89204-661-9

ACKNOWLEDGEMENTS

It starts with a simple idea and snowballs into a major project with important contributions from many sources. Not only does a book offer words, photographs and information, it showcases behind-the-scenes skills of special people who plan, edit, proofread, gather, design, process and participate in ways too numerous to list. These are dedicated people who value quality and are willing to work beyond their weekly obligations to achieve it.

Start with editorial director Steve Meyerhoff, who always provides the direction and encouragement that keeps projects like this on an even keel, and senior editor Joe Hoppel, who makes everything he touches better with his editing ability and extensive sports knowledge. The outstanding photographs that make this book special were gathered by Albert Dickson and Peter Newcomb, who also contributed their own photos to the project.

The book's design was created and executed by Matt Kindt, with special input from prepress director Bob Parajon and correction help from Christen Sager. The lively photographic reproduction reflects the work of prepress specialist Chris Barnes-Amaro with special assists from Steve Romer and David Brickey.

It's difficult to imagine how the editorial portraits of football weekends at the 20 selected universities could have been executed without the help and advice of TSN college football experts Tom Dienhart and Matt Hayes and the input of fans and employees from the various schools. A special thanks to the following people for their time and patience:

Alabama—Barry Allen, Kenneth Gaddy, Daniel Hopper; Army—Bob Beretta, Mady Salvani; Auburn— Janet Hill, Charles McGairty, Stephen Naughton, Sara Waid; Clemson—Sam Blackman, Tim Bourret; Florida—Doug Brown, Jon McBride; Florida State—Doug Mannheimer, Rob Wilson; Georgia—Claude Felton, Freddy Jones, Larry Munson, N.J. Tippens; LSU—Jim Hawthorne, Ricky Suprean; Michigan—Brian Akre, Perry Calandrino; Nebraska— Mike Babcock, Don Bryant, Rick Schwieger; Notre Dame—Todd Fitzpatrick, Terese Meyerhoff, Pete Ugo; Ohio State—Raimund Goerler, Jack Park, Fred Zimmerman; Oklahoma—Danny Davis, Matt Trantham; Penn State—Jeff Nelson, Lou Prato; USC—Tony Fox, Don Ludwig, Ron Orr, Tim Tessalone; Texas—John Bianco, Bill Little, Emilie Williams-Fennell; Texas A&M—Alan Cannon, Simon Gonzalez; Tennessee—Haywood Harris, Mike Strange; Washington—Jim Daves, Dick Erickson, Leslie Wurzberger; Wisconsin—Justin Doherty, Wayne Esser, Mike Lorenz.

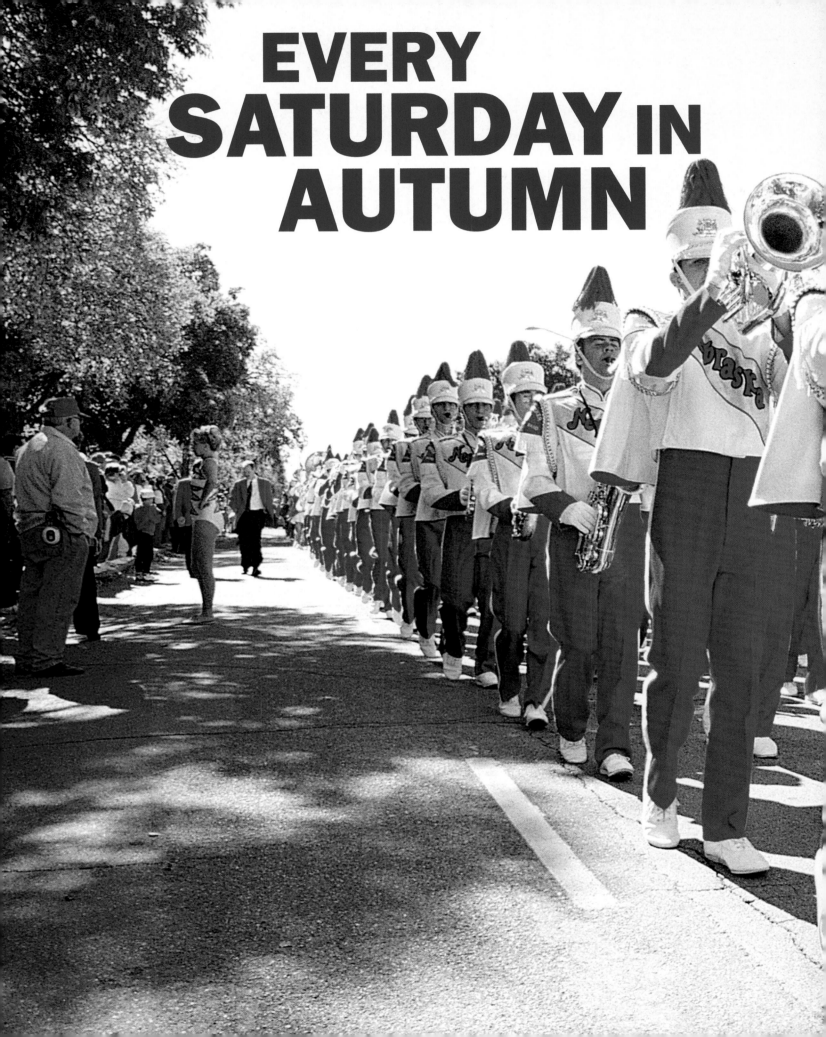

EVERY SATURDAY IN AUTUMN

C O N T E N T S

FOREWORD

Craig James, a record-setting high school running back out of Houston, grew up in the shadow of Southwest Conference football and the then-dominant Texas program of Darrell Royal. James went on to college stardom as part of SMU's "Pony Express" running tandem with Eric Dickerson and played seven professional seasons, one as a Pro Bowl back for the New England Patriots. James spent five years as part of ESPN's College GameDay team with Chris Fowler and Lee Corso and now works as a game analyst for CBS.

Let me give you the definition of a perfect Saturday. I wake up in time to catch College GameDay on ESPN. Chris Fowler and company fill me in on all of the news and notes about the games happening throughout the day. Then I watch Notre Dame battle USC, Florida take on Georgia, Nebraska try to hold off Oklahoma and Ohio State try to figure out a way to beat Michigan. Each game comes down to the fourth quarter and a final drive.

For dessert, I go to Auburn-Alabama. Look up the word "intensity" in the dictionary and they have this game listed as a footnote. By the time it ends, I'm pooped—but not too tired to catch the scoreboard show.

College football represents a lot of things to a lot of people. For me, it brings back childhood memories of Lindsey Nelson saying hello from the Cotton Bowl on January 1. Or Keith Jackson shouting out one of his trademark expressions. The vision of Bear Bryant and Joe Paterno walking the sideline is real to me. Sitting at Kyle Field and being part of a Twelfth Man tradition that is so special at Texas A&M. Seeing Miami-Florida State, or Florida-Florida State, is hard to beat, too.

I have a bond with the game and its history. As a boy growing up in Texas, I used to listen to University of Texas football games. The Southwest Conference was a powerhouse then, and Texas was coached by Darrell Royal and featured players like Steve Worster, James Street and Cotton Speyer. The Longhorns playing on Saturday afternoon was as big a deal as the Dallas Cowboys playing on Sunday.

My athletic talent eventually allowed me to become a blue-chip prospect out of high school and just about everybody recruited me, including Texas. But coach Royal had retired and it just didn't seem like the same team. So I passed on the scholarship offer and went to Southern Methodist. Eight months later, there I was playing UT at Texas Stadium. I remember the game like it was yesterday. I went on the field for pregame and I'm standing in the end zone when the University of Texas team comes out. The Longhorn band cranks up the UT fight song and, well, I bend over and throw up. It's the only time I got that nervous before a game I participated in. And we got our butts kicked!

It's funny the effect different places can have on you. As a player, going to Texas, Texas A&M or Arkansas were the ultimate highs. Many players feared going on the road, but I looked forward to it because of the energy I got from opposing fans. And the realization that I was playing on fields of teams I had grown up listening to made all those games extra special.

Now I get those feelings for different reasons. How can you top the mystique and aura you feel every time you go to Notre Dame? There is a special feeling when Notre Dame is playing Florida State, or Michigan. You can feel the intensity of the crowd and there is really something about that sacred field. It's unbelievable just standing there knowing about all the wonderful games that have been played there. And sure enough, in the fourth quarter something always happens in those big games and Notre Dame is able to pull it out.

That's the beauty of college football—every place is different. The passion of the South is unparalleled. There's no question about the intensity at Florida, Georgia, Alabama, Auburn, LSU—they love football in the South. But Midwest fans also love the game and they show up in huge numbers to support their teams. And the Pac-10 is a very undervalued, underappreciated league.

It's all great fun, no matter where you go. I've been really lucky because I have been able to experience the great game of college football on two levels—as a player at the major college level and as a broadcaster who could soak up some of the sport's flavor and pageantry. For years, one way or another, college football has been a major part of my life.

You might say I have lived out my dream.

Craig James

EVERY SATURDAY IN
AUTUMN

Every Saturday in autumn, they swarm onto college campuses like hungry locusts, intensely loyal fans starving for football fulfillment and ready to devour all the color, pageantry and excitement they can find. They are young and old, male and female, rich alumni and poor students—normally well-adjusted folks who get swept away by a madness that permeates colleges and universities from coast to coast.

Theirs is a harmless but incurable disease, diagnosed by such symptoms as unconscionable color coordination, painted cars and faces, decorated motor homes, flag-waving pride, chest-thumping professions of deep love and an uncontrollable desire to discuss football and cook something on a grill. They yell inspirational battle cries like "War Eagle," "Roll Tide" and "Go Blue." They make curious chomping motions with their arms, hump their bodies to get maximum volume out of special yells and flash familiar signals with their hands.

On every Saturday in autumn, inhibition gives way to an overt passion that has existed as long as there has been college football.

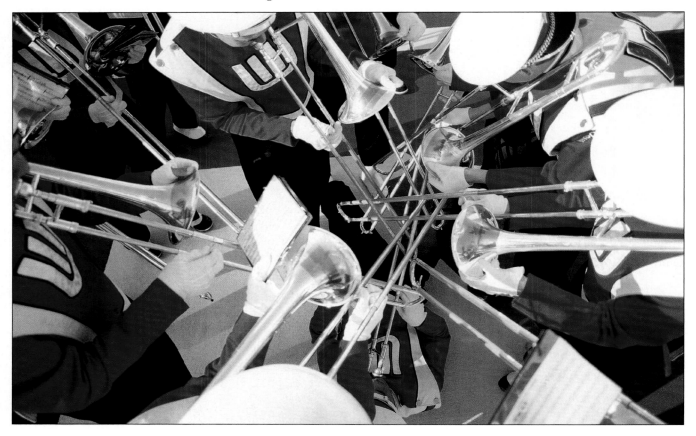

The pageantry of college football, which separates it from other team sports, is built around the creativity of marching bands.

"Keith always says there are four generations of fans in the stands at college football games," says ABC-TV game analyst Bob Griese, referring to longtime partner and college football guru Keith Jackson. "That's what makes (college games) special. They're different from the pros with their tradition, the mascots, tailgating, the fight songs, the bands before the game and at half-time.

"Even the cheerleaders are different, much more acrobatic and showy. The pageantry of college football is great."

So are the traditions, blind passion, sense of participation and electric stadium atmosphere that provide an almost mystical backdrop for the game itself. Every football Saturday becomes a many-faceted event—equal parts festival, celebration, party, competition and religious experience. It's a deeply rooted piece of Americana, with some very special trimmings.

From the midnight yell practice at Texas A&M to the Purple Cow mascot at Williams College, every school has its long-practiced rituals. Wins and losses might measure the heart of every football program, but tradition measures its soul. It comes in the form of stories, beliefs and customs handed off and passed down from generation to generation.

Like playing between the hedges at Georgia, rubbing Howard's Rock at Clemson and visiting the Grotto at Notre Dame. Tennessee has its Volunteer Navy, Oklahoma has a Sooner Schooner and Colorado runs with the Buffalo—literally. At Auburn, they decorate Toomer's Corner and at Ohio State they dot the "i."

"Traditions are what separates college football from pro football," says Kirk Herbstreit, a former Ohio State quarterback and current College GameDay analyst for ESPN. "They are unique and special and every team has its own. I love that part of the game and you can't help but have a strong passion for the incredible things you see.

"Traditions are passed down from generation to generation. As alumni, you have a love affair with the team because that's your place. Students know that their grandparents and parents went to school there and experienced many of the same things. Now it's their turn. It's their first chance to experience all the things they've been told about."

Some traditions, like the Script Ohio band routine that Ohio State introduced in 1936, have changed little over the years. Others have evolved from a simple beginning to a more elaborate present, like the Tommy Trojan tradition that was unveiled in the form of a 1930 statue at USC and expanded in 1961 to a Tommy Trojan-like figure who rides a white horse at games. When Chief Osceola was introduced to Florida State fans in 1978, he simply led the Seminoles onto the field on his Appaloosa horse. Now he charges to midfield and spikes a flaming spear in a choreographed pregame show at Doak Campbell Stadium.

The Big Red Shop, once a Nebraska football institution, went out of business after the 2000 season.

Still other traditions have disappeared or diminished, victims of stadium renovations and corporate dealings. The Spirit of Troy Band's annual march down the Coliseum's peristyle before USC games against UCLA or Notre Dame, an impressive sight, has lost much of its impact because of recently constructed field-level end zone seats that block much of the view. The memorabilia-selling Big Red Shop, a Nebraska institution for years, closed its doors after the 2000 season. The "Track People" are only a hazy memory to most fans at Georgia.

"Back in the '70s, when I was coaching, we had the Track People," says Vince Dooley, who won 201 games in 25 years as Bulldogs coach and still serves as the school's athletic director. "There would be about 15,000 who would gather on the railroad tracks and watch the game for free. The tracks were on the east end of Sanford Stadium, which was open in the '70s.

"They took great pride in being the Track People and the TV would always photograph them when it did games at Georgia. They would bring sofas and mattresses and spend the night right there along the tracks. Of course, they would have to get up and move when a train came by.

When we decided to renovate and close that area (of the stadium), they came to us with a petition signed by 10,000 people, letting us know how important this was. They were really something."

So is the Cockaboose Railroad, a South Carolina tailgating tradition that started in 1990. And night football, an LSU staple since 1931. But for dramatic impact, crowd-pleasing excitement and good, old-fashioned showmanship, nothing can match a team's well-choreographed game-day entrance from a dark stadium tunnel.

"The whole Michigan atmosphere is pretty exciting," says Bo Schembechler, who walked the Michigan Stadium tunnel many times during his 21 years (1969-89) as Wolverines coach. "The stadium is unique, so large, and that tunnel. There's nothing like coming out of that darkness, suddenly it's light and all hell breaks loose. You never get tired of that experience and you never forget it."

Costumed mascots, like Notre Dame's Leprechaun (below), have become fixtures at football stadiums around the country.

Tommie Frazier, who quarterbacked Nebraska to consecutive national championships in 1994 and '95, didn't make the Cornhuskers' famed Tunnel Walk as many times as Schembechler walked the Michigan tunnel, but the impact was no less inspiring. And every step was watched on a giant video board by fans packed into Memorial Stadium.

"You know as you're walking down the tunnel that the fans are visualizing you and seeing your every move," says Frazier. "When you hit the field, it's like entering another world. The place just explodes. Those fans are something. You know they'll support you. You want to give them your best, go out and win the game."

Traditions are a source of inspiration and many coaches use them as emotional weapons to whip teams into a game-day frenzy. That frenzy often intimidates opponents, many of whom cannot match the emotional intensity.

"As the visiting coach, you try to block all that stuff out," says Frazier, who returned to Nebraska in 2000 as a Baylor assistant and experienced the Tunnel Walk from the other side. "You have to show the players that it doesn't matter to you, that you will just do your job, that it doesn't affect you. But you can't block everything.

"They (the Baylor players) saw the atmosphere and they were in awe. They were nervous because they had never seen anything like that. You can prepare 'em all week, tell them over and over what to expect, but until they're actually in that situation, they won't fully understand."

If you want aura and mystique, go to Notre Dame, Michigan, Army or USC for a football weekend. Head to Nebraska for friendly and to Washington or Brigham Young for scenic. Go south if you're looking for in-your-face, take-no-prisoners fervor and passion.

"The South is more intense," says Lee Corso, a former Florida State player who works with Herbstreit as an ESPN College GameDay analyst. "Football is really important to those people. Games there are tremendously different in atmosphere. There is nothing like Southern football—the passion for teams. And every single one of those programs (in the Southeastern Conference) has that passion."

Herbstreit agrees. "I think football is almost a cult following in the South," he says. "The Big Ten is more traditional, more of an old-guard mentality. Ohio State and Wisconsin are SEC schools in the Big Ten. Ohio State fans are lunatics. ... it's a much more hostile atmosphere than at Michigan."

Passion can be measured in many ways. Penn State fans love their tailgating, Texas A&M cherishes its traditions and Wisconsin jives to its Fifth Quarter band concert. Although Ohio State

fans might be more vocal and confrontational, Michigan Stadium has attracted more than 100,000 fans for every game since 1975. The Swamp at Florida is one of the most intimidating venues in the country because of rabid Gator fans, but more respectful Nebraskans have filled Memorial Stadium for every home game since 1962. Lincoln is special, a place where opponents lose with grace and dignity.

Atmosphere is everything in college football and a lot of it is generated on the sidelines.

"The best place of all to watch college football is Nebraska," says Corso, who served as head coach at Indiana for 10 seasons, at Louisville for four and at Northern Illinois for one. "They are the best college fans in America, bar none. Forget the Tunnel Walk and everything else, they appreciate and respect the way college football is played and they show it constantly, both for the Cornhuskers and their opponents. The fans there are the best."

Griese likes Nebraska because of what he calls sportsmanship. "I remember watching Washington beat Nebraska at Lincoln in 1991," he says, "and the fans cheered the Huskies as they went off the field. Nobody was yelling and complaining about the Cornhuskers losing. I've been back several times since and that's always the case."

The passion also shows in the way Nebraska travels. Notre Dame officials were startled when Cornhuskers fans made a 2000 pilgrimage to South Bend, bought every ticket they could find

Whether you venture to see Georgia or any other team on a fall Saturday, chances are you'll find a lot more than football being played.

and turned the traditionally blue-and-gold Notre Dame Stadium red. Washington had a similar experience when Nebraska played at Seattle in 1997, and Big 12 Conference cities always prepare for the Big Red wave.

Tennessee fans might not travel as well as Cornhuskers, but they do know how to put on a show. From the tailgating, Vol Navy and Vol Walk traditions to the surround-sound passion of huge Neyland Stadium, it's atmosphere with an orange tint.

"If you're talking about the best place to watch one game," Corso says, "go to Tennessee at night. The lights, that huge stadium, Rocky Top—there is no better thrill. For noise and intimidation, go to The Swamp at Gainesville. Saturday night at LSU is really something. But for pure college atmosphere, Tennessee is the place."

But not the only place. Herbstreit made his first visit to Kyle Field at College Station, Texas, in 2000 and came away impressed.

"I grew up in the Big Ten and I love SEC football, but my visit to Texas A&M last year was phenomenal," he says. "The students there are absolutely incredible. They are the Twelfth Man, such a huge part of every game. They're so loud you can't hear yourself think. I loved it there. It's a unique spot to watch college football."

Frazier offers a different perspective. "College Station is a good environment," he says, "but it's nothing like Nebraska. The toughest place I ever played was Washington. The way that stadium is built, the crowd noise, the stomping, the rowdiness of the fans—they're always in the game. It was very loud."

Herbstreit and Corso agree, but they also will tell you Washington is not the loudest venue in the Pacific-10 Conference. That honor belongs now to Oregon's 41,698-seat Autzen Stadium—Corso's pick as the loudest arena per person in America.

Loud is proud, but USC has other ways to measure Pac-10 passion. One is fan devotion, which is epitomized by the legacy of former USC worshiper Giles Pellerin, a cardinal-and-gold fixture at the Los Angeles Coliseum dating back to 1926.

Old, young or in between, football Saturdays offer a little something for everyone.

The amazing Pellerin visited 75 stadiums in 50 cities and witnessed a staggering 797 consecutive USC games. The king of all super fans died in 1998, at age 91, while watching his beloved Trojans play rival UCLA at the Rose Bowl.

From Notre Dame's Friday night pep rally to Wisconsin's lively Fifth Quarter concert at Camp Randall Stadium, bands control the pace, mood and pageantry of a college football weekend. They march, dance, jive, serenade and perform complicated, choreographed maneuvers that give fall Saturdays their festive atmosphere.

It's hard to imagine football without its background music. Fight songs, popular rock tunes, stirring marches and showy dance routines keep everything at a feverish pitch and the cheerleaders, mascots and technology-enhanced pregame shows give the day a theatrical flair.

Go to a Wisconsin or USC game and watch how two of the country's most creative marching bands control the day's festive pace, from on-campus pregame activities to stadium postgame concerts that have generated national attention. The Notre Dame band, with its colorful Irish Guard, performs and parades with spirit-raising fervor and there's nothing like the musical sparks that fly, out of the spotlight, of course, whenever longtime rivals hook up in their annual grudge match.

"Boy, do I remember the electricity of Ohio State and Michigan when I was coaching," Schembechler recalls. "Whether you played in Columbus or Ann Arbor, the two best bands in the country were competing against each other as well."

Southern University and Grambling State fans would argue that the "two best bands in the country" lock drums annually in the Friday night Battle of the Bands before the Bayou Classic in New Orleans. The historically black colleges are nationally renowned for their non-traditional shows—hip, soulful journeys into rhythm-and-blues.

Other bands depend less on marching and choreography and more on satire and fun-poking humor.

For pom pom-waving Alabama fans, there's nothing sweeter than a victory over hated-rival Auburn.

Stanford's "scatter" band has been antagonizing school officials and insulting opposing fans for years with its irreverent, satire-filled programs. So have the bands at all Ivy League schools, which are more interested in social commentary than cross-campus marches and pregame concerts.

The game-day atmosphere has other interesting enhancements. Many schools juice it up with live mascots—some wild and intimidating, others trained to perform with crowd-pleasing panache. Georgia has Uga, Texas has Bevo and Texas A&M has Reveille. Mike the Tiger is an intimidating presence at LSU and Ralphie the Buffalo stampedes around Colorado's Folsom Field. You have to look up to see Tiger, Auburn's high-flying War Eagle, and Mach 1, Air Force's performing falcon. Traveler and Renegade offer fans a ride on the wild side at USC and Florida State.

But nothing can stir the blood more than that annual battle against a hated opponent. Emotions are higher, the sense of urgency is stronger, the buildup is bigger and victory is a lot more important when you're trying to beat a rival, both on the field and off.

"The best game for pageantry, the game you would go to if you were going to see one game, is Army-Navy," says Corso. "The Midshipmen parading in, the color and tradition, the excitement, there is nothing like it anywhere. When they used to play at John F. Kennedy Stadium (Philadelphia), I would get goosebumps."

Others might choose Auburn-Alabama, Nebraska-Oklahoma, Texas-Texas A&M, Alabama-Tennessee, Florida-Florida State, USC-UCLA, Clemson-South Carolina, Missouri-Kansas, Purdue-Indiana, Mississippi-Mississippi State—the list is endless. And all have that life-and-death undertone. Schembechler recalls his almost legendary battles against Woody Hayes and Ohio State.

"When I coached, that game was for the championship of the Big Ten," he says. "Almost every year, we were playing for the Rose Bowl. Once that 10th game (of the season) was over, Ohio State week would come up and every day the electricity got thicker. I'm sure that was true in Columbus as well.

"That game—we did something to prepare for Ohio State every day of the season. You looked ahead because you could never get that game out of your mind. Woody was such a character ... and, I guess, so was I. With two coaches that way, well it was fun."

Fun, as in crazy—a kind of crazy that is hard to find at any other kind of sports venue. The flags, the aroma of cooking food, homemade banners, exploding cannons, buzzing planes, excited chatter, contagious laughter, colorful decorations and clothes, marching bands, special costumes, an air of expectancy, ear-shattering noise, passion and intensity—the joy of victory, the agony of defeat.

Every Saturday in autumn.

The fan intensity at Florida Field carries over to the players, who seldom lose and always entertain.

I t's a charming blend of color, tradition and pageantry, a sport that measures success by off-field passion as well as victories. Nothing inspires that passion like college football and no other sport can match its consuming electricity and fervor.

College football is not just a game—it's an event, celebrated on fall Saturdays by the most dedicated and loyal fans in America. They come in color-coordinated armies and suck up the atmosphere of tailgate parties and marching bands while reliving the traditions that give the sport its special personality.

Game-day tradition and passion is difficult to measure, but that didn't stop a panel of football writers, editors and radio analysts at *The Sporting News* from putting together a poll rating the 20 best places to spend a college football weekend. It's a subjective ranking that looks at the fun side of the game—the most colorful traditions, the most festive atmospheres and the greatest outpouring of emotion that you'll find anywhere, before any game.

The sections that follow offer game-day portraits of the 20 schools included in TSN's poll. This is the other side of college football, the game as seen through red, orange, blue, scarlet, gold, purple and crimson-colored glasses.

Every Saturday in Autumn · Tennessee Volunteers

TENNESSEE

VOLUNTEERS

They come by air, land and water to spread the gospel of Tennessee football. They blind you with their orange passion, impress you with their undying devotion and sweep you away with their infectious enthusiasm. When you venture into the shadow of the Great Smoky Mountains on a crisp autumn weekend, be prepared to experience unconditional love, unadulterated frenzy and an overdose of the popular 1967 song "Rocky Top."

For the University of Tennessee fan, football is not an activity—it's a way of life. Its magnitude is incredible and its message is far-reaching, passed from generation to generation, from neighbor to neighbor every day at grocery stores, laundromats, banks, schools, churches and airports throughout the state—and beyond. When more than 100,000 people descend in an orange wave on Knoxville for a typical Volunteer home game, it's difficult not to get swept away by its festive intensity.

This is the world of checkerboard end zones, the Power T, a Volunteer Navy, the Vol Walk and Smokey, the school's coon hound mascot. It's also home to one of the biggest, baddest stadiums in all of football and an in-your-face winning legacy to match.

Orange, sunshine and passion are the three constants at every Tennessee game.

If you build it, they will come." The words were not written about Tennessee's Neyland Stadium, but they certainly could have been. The home of the Volunteers, dedicated as Shields-Watkins Field in 1921 with 3,200 seats, has endured 17 expansions to rank as the second-largest facility in college football with a capacity of more than 104,000. Every one of those seats will be filled on a football Saturday.

So will standing-room areas, which explains the record 108,768 crowd the Vols drew for a 2000 thriller against Florida. They have averaged more than 106,000 since 1996, and thousands of other fans typically come to soak up the atmosphere, unable to find tickets. Tennessee football fervor runs so deep that 73,000 once turned out for a spring game.

Perfect attendance makes for difficult logistics. The crush of 90,000 visitors—many of them crammed into Knoxville hotels—and the shoehorning of thousands of orange-decorated motor homes and vehicles into a campus with limited parking quickly became something of a nightmare, so many fans now arrive as early as Thursday and settle in for a long party-filled weekend without the prospect of fighting those legendary Saturday morning traffic jams.

The traffic got so bad in 1962 that former Vols broadcaster George Mooney found an alternative route to Neyland Stadium, navigating his little runabout down the Tennessee River and parking it a few hundred yards from his gate. Other Volunteer fans admired his ingenuity and followed suit. Now, almost four decades later, more than 200 boats, ranging from small motor crafts to yachts and cruisers, traverse the river as part of the giant flotilla Tennessee has dubbed its Volunteer Navy.

Tennessee football is about that level of participation as much as winning and losing ... It's not a stretch to say football, Tennessee style, is beyond important.

When tied up at one of the river's numerous docks, boats become part of a giant floating tailgate party, which will feature food, food and more food, ranging from snacks to three- and four-course dinners. Tailgating at Tennessee, whether on land or water, is a social event, often planned out well in advance. Vacations are scheduled around football games; so are weddings, business trips and even the birth of babies.

The Volunteer Navy has become so fashionable that fans make the trip to Knoxville just for

Players, ready to rumble, run out of the tunnel into packed Neyland Stadium during an emotional and stirring pregame entrance.

The Volunteer
Navy turns
into a color-
ful tailgating
army (above)
on Saturdays
during foot-
ball season.

the festivities. They party, enjoy the campus and retire to their below-deck air-conditioning and recliner, all set to watch the game on their big-screen TV.

Tennessee football is about that level of participation as much as winning and losing, although a rare Volunteer home loss might suggest otherwise. Knoxville businessmen will tell you about how this city of about 180,000 goes into a funk after a Tennessee loss, about the tender psyche of obsessed fans who mope through the following week. It's not a stretch to say football, Tennessee style, is beyond important.

It doesn't hurt that the campus is part of a scenic masterpiece, cradled to the south by the Tennessee River, bordered on the southeast by the Smokies and dominated to the east by the impressive Knoxville skyline. With the leaves changing colors, the smoke hanging over the mountains and a golden glow emanating from Knoxville's high-rising Sunsphere tower (the city's 1982 World's Fair landmark), this looks like the work of a divine paintbrush.

While the campus lacks the small-town charm of an Auburn or a Clemson, it more than makes up for its shortcomings with its beautiful setting. Once centered on top of a plateau known as The Hill, the campus has expanded west, carving its identity out of residential streets while integrating nicely with the city life of Knoxville.

On Friday nights before games, alumni will swarm into the city to search out that perfect eating establishment or nightclub. The students head for The Strip, a popular area on West Cumberland Avenue—the northern border of campus. Football is the backdrop for a night of revelry that merely stokes anticipation. By early Saturday morning, grills and ovens will be fired up and the sweet aroma of cooking food will waft through the waking campus, followed closely by the first sounds of cheerful banter. The electricity is unmistakable and contagious.

These are people who know how to tailgate. While food and beverage are being consumed in great quantities on the waterfront, land lovers tantalize new arrivals with their well-planned menus and activities. Tennessee football is the focus of conversation and players, opponents and game plans are analyzed, adjusted, dissected and critiqued many times by many fans who, by virtue of unflagging loyalty, feel a vested connection to the team's immediate and long-range fortunes.

By noon before a 3:30 game, the campus is packed with touring alumni and thousands more are arriving on the hundreds of buses that deliver them from off-campus locations. Many fan out to visit old haunts and revive old friendships. Others will make mandatory stops at the bookstore and Hall of Fame, where they can pay proper tribute to the school's long winning tradition. But the real fun begins about two hours before game time when thousands of fans, who have been lining Volunteer Boulevard and Peyton Manning Pass for hours, participate in a Tennessee-style lovefest that has become known as the Vol Walk.

It doesn't get any better than this for a college football player. From Gibbs Hall to the Stadium, team members stroll casually through a corridor of orange worshipers, accepting their well-meaning

Among the traditions that set Tennessee apart from other programs are fans arriving by boat (left), the players' parade-like walk to the stadium (right) and the band's Power T formation (top).

For pure pageantry and showmanship, the Pride of the Southland Band is hard to beat. But Smokey, the blue tick coon hound that serves as Tennessee's mascot, is No. 1 in the heart of Volunteer fans.

pats on the back and soaking in their words of encouragement and unrestrained adulation. For these few, brief, shining moments, the players are the center of the Tennessee universe, warriors about to do battle for a righteous cause. The only thing missing is ticker tape.

While the Vol Walk triggers a genuine outpouring of emotion, the Pride of the Southland Band brings football to an even more feverish pitch an hour later with its peppy five-block march from the Band Room to the Stadium. Again fans line the route and this time they respond frenetically to the Tennessee fight songs and, of course, the first renditions of that adopted crowd favorite.

"Wish that I was on ol' Rocky Top, down in the Tennessee hills. ..." The words will be repeated with out-of-tune delight, over and over in the next few hours, by more people than you could ever imagine gathered together in one place.

Former Vols star and coach Johnny Majors (left) with Alabama coaching legend Bear Bryant.

From field level, the seats rise quickly, creating a football canyon with the highest point of the facility towering 202 feet above. The double-decked bowl is expansive beyond imagination, a reflection of the long-successful football program developed and nurtured for 3½ decades by former coaching legend and athletic director Gen. Robert R. Neyland.

This is a stadium that both inspires and intimidates. First-time opponents, making their Friday walk-through, marvel at the expanse, their straining eyes focusing upward in obvious awe. Longtime fans share that feeling, preferring to focus on memories of Neyland, Johnny and Bobby Majors, Carl Pickens, Heath

From checkerboard end zones at Neyland Stadium to streets bearing the names of football heroes, tradition and memories are constantly on display at Tennessee.

Shuler, Peyton Manning and many other greats who have contributed to 13 Southeastern Conference titles and two undisputed national championships.

When filled to the brim, Neyland Stadium is overwhelming. On a sunny afternoon, don't forget your sunglasses because the orange reflection can be blinding. Sportswriters tell stories of fan roars that shake the press box, perched on the west upper rim. To the players on the field, this mass of humanity looms large and loud, a natural surround sound without any need for amplifiers or speakers.

The orange-and-white checkerboard end zones add a special flavor to the proceedings, as does one of the most celebrated player entrances in college football. Everyone is seated, the crowd is properly juiced and anticipation is at its feverish peak when showtime officially arrives.

After a six-minute pregame prep is followed by playing of the national anthem, the 300-plus-member band marches to the north end zone where it forms the famed Power T—a T-shaped formation that stretches from end zone to the 50-yard line, its long stem lined up with the Tennessee locker room tunnel. When Smokey VIII, the cheerleaders and the entire Volunteer

Two names that live on in Tennessee football lore: Gen. Robert R. Neyland (above) and Peyton Manning.

team dash madly through the human corridor, the crowd lets out a goosebump-raising roar that sets the tone for three hours of football.

"If you're an athlete, there's no place on earth better than this place," said the appropriately named Tee Martin, quarterback of the Vols' 1998 national champs. And for both players and fans, the luster never wears off.

Neyland
Stadium stands
like a foot-
ball fortress
overlooking
the Tennessee
River.

Smokey became a revered member of the Vol family in 1953, when a blue tick coon hound owned by Rev. Bill Brooks won the heart of the Neyland Stadium crowd with an unexpected burst of showmanship. The original Smokey was one of several dogs introduced to fans during

a mascot-selection process. When his name was called, Smokey threw back his head and barked. The fans cheered and he barked again ... and again until the place was in an uproar. The verdict was sealed.

That was eight Smokeys ago in a line of decendants supplied by Brooks and his wife. For almost a half century, the dogs have enjoyed football from their special end zone perspective, spicing up festivities occasionally by nipping at opposing cheerleaders and mascots. If Smokey is awed by the surroundings, it doesn't show. He doesn't even seem to mind that his prerecorded growl is played over the public address system whenever the Volunteers score.

That growl has become joyously familiar to Tennessee fans, who have watched their team post

a sparkling 68-8 home record since 1989. More than 100,000 people going crazy, coupled with a storied tradition, makes for a successful formula. More subtle traditions are front and center on game day, too:

• The famed orange "T" on both sides of the Tennessee helmet.

• The silly-but-popular quips of public address announcer Bobby Denton.

• The sight and sound of 100,000 fans singing and swaying to the strains of Rocky Top.

• George Bitzas, a talented tenor, who belted out a powerful national anthem until his retirement after the 2000 season.

When you visit Knoxville, don't duck out at halftime and miss the show by the Pride of the Southland Band, one of the best musical groups in the land. The band has represented the university at numerous presidential inaugurations, every major bowl game and many other important functions. Its halftime shows will often have a theme—how 'bout a country hoedown?—and some have even featured such singers as Lee Greenwood and Charley Pride.

When the game ends, the party continues. Many fans don't leave Knoxville on Saturday night because of the traffic congestion, so tailgate activities resume, hopefully coupled with a victory celebration. The mass exodus actually gets underway on Sunday morning, when Knoxville regains a semblance of normalcy—for a few days at least.

Until that next home game arrives and some of the most colorful fans in college football revisit ol' Rocky Top.

Every Saturday in Autumn · Notre Dame Fighting Irish

NOTRE DAME

FIGHTING IRISH

You can't escape that almost mystical aura, a sense that heroic people have performed legendary feats on these hallowed grounds. You can't ignore the imposing tradition, the boundless energy, the defiant confidence or the suspected connection this place has with forces beyond. Notre Dame, on a crisp, autumn Saturday afternoon, reels you in with its simple charms and then goes out of its way to overwhelm you.

Blame it on the Golden Dome, the stately crown atop the administration building that ranks among the most recognized sports symbols in the world. Or blame it on Touchdown Jesus, Fair Catch Corby, the Grotto, Notre Dame Stadium, Knute Rockne, the Four Horsemen, George Gipp, Ara Parseghian and any of the numerous All-Americans and Heisman Trophy winners who have lifted Fighting Irish football into the international consciousness.

When you make that first drive down Notre Dame Avenue, take that first step on paths once walked by Paul Hornung and Joe Montana or experience the infectious, obsessive enthusiasm

The stadium is one of many tributes to the past at Notre Dame, where tradition is king.

for Notre Dame on a football weekend, you've entered a dimension that only a select few sports venues can match.

"If you could find a way to bottle the Notre Dame spirit, you could light up the universe," former Fighting Irish quarterback Joe Theismann once observed. And, deep down, you suspect he's right.

Anybody who sets foot on the South Bend campus, a football oasis on the northern edge of Indiana's basketball madness, is quickly immersed in the legends of Rockne, Gipp, the

Horsemen and, of course, the most impressive string of national championship teams in college football history. Students are indoctrinated with legends of grandeur and other verbal reminders of a rich football heritage; visitors cannot escape the nationally recognized football landmarks, many of them religious statues and symbols placed strategically around the tree-lined campus of the 159-year-old Catholic university.

Few students complete their freshman year without intimate knowledge of *Knute Rockne, All-American*, a must-view movie that captures the football passion of the former Notre Dame player (1910-13) and coach (1918-30) who guided the Irish to the first three of 11 national titles and set in motion many of the traditions that still fuel the football program today. At some point during their South Bend stay, students will pay homage to the coaching genius of Frank Leahy, Parseghian, Dan Devine and Lou Holtz, be inspired by the story of former Fighting Irish player Rudy Ruettiger, whose indomitable spirit was immortalized in a 1993 film, and pay poetic tribute to the Gipper and sportswriter Grantland Rice, who in 1924 penned the immortal words, "Outlined against a blue-gray October sky, the Four Horsemen rode again. ..."

The Notre Dame experience is generational, passed through families like precious heirlooms.

Freshmen are well advised to memorize the words to the Alma Mater and Victory March because they will be asked to "Wake up the echoes" thousands of times over the next four years.

Visual football images have become a more overt feature of the Notre Dame fabric. Every day, at different points on the tightly knit campus, students pass symbols that have become passionately associated with Fighting Irish football.

On the south wall of the 14-story Hesburgh Library, a 132-foot-high stone mosaic depicts Jesus Christ, his arms upraised, teaching a gathering of apostles, saints and scholars. The mural, visible from certain points inside nearby Notre Dame Stadium, has become known as Touchdown Jesus. Across campus stands Fair Catch Corby, a statue depicting former university president Rev. William J. Corby, his hand upraised while giving absolution to the Irish

Touchdown Jesus oversees football and other matters from the south wall of Hesburgh Library.

The Grotto, a
stone-covered
shrine on the
edge of cam-
pus, offers
special inspi-
ration to
football visi-
tors.

Brigade during the Civil War battle of Gettysburg. "We're No. 1 Moses" stands in flowing robes on the west side of the library, pointing skyward while chastising wayward Israelites that there is only one God.

No visit to Notre Dame is complete without a side trip to the Grotto, a stone-covered shrine to Our Lady of Lourdes on the edge of campus near St. Mary's and St. Joseph's lakes. The Grotto, a mandatory stop for Holtz on game mornings during his 11-year coaching tenure, provides kneelers and candles to light for players and fans seeking special inspiration.

Tributes to the past are everywhere, but none more conspicuous than 80,232-seat Notre Dame Stadium. Rockne helped design the single-decked oval structure before it opened in 1930 and it was expanded from 59,075 to its current capacity before the 1997 campaign. A yellow-brick facade encloses the original red-brick outer wall, which remains as a sentimental reminder.

Notre Dame is a lifesize picture postcard, with leaves changing color, band playing and such classic architecture as the Golden Dome and Basilica steeple forming a stately backdrop. This is a campus where the alumni always return and the 10,000-plus students (most of whom live on campus) seldom leave. That special bond makes it easy to spread the football message.

Most students make the Friday night pep rally the starting point of their football weekend ritual—and it usually provides a loud and raucous framework for everything that follows. The rally before the 1997 rededication of expanded Notre Dame Stadium packed in 35,000 wild and crazy fans. A more typical rally now takes place at the Joyce Athletic and Convocation Center (the JACC), where standing-room crowds gather and late-arriving fans often have to be turned away.

The pep rally, which has gained national exposure on ESPN, is an hour-long cascade of emotion-triggering music (the electrifying Victory March and Alma Mater) and motivational rhetoric. The music is provided by the oldest continuous-existence university band in the country; speeches are delivered with fitting vigor by a special guest, two current players and the Notre Dame coach.

Stories still circulate about the late-1960s guest appearance at a Parseghian-staged rally of balding actor Pat O'Brien, who had played Rockne in the movie three decades earlier. "Go out there and crack 'em, crack 'em, crack 'em, crack 'em," an inspired O'Brien exhorted, ignoring the din of exploding firecrackers. "Fight to live. Fight to win. Win, win, win, win. ..." More recent guests, alums such as Phil Donahue, Regis Philbin and George Wendt, have had a tough act to follow.

Friday nights are usually spent in such mood-setting local hangouts as

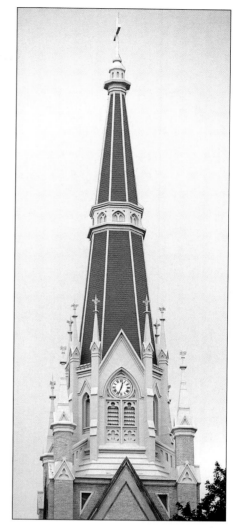

'We're No. 1 Moses'(left) and 'Fair Catch Corby'(right) stand prominently on campus, ready to address both religious and football matters. Prominent in the Notre Dame skyline is the stately Basilica steeple (top right).

The Band of the Fighting Irish provides a spirited pregame warmup for the emotional players' entrance.

Coach's ("Ara Parseghian, table for six!"), The Linebacker and the Senior Bar. But revelers beware: Game-day wakeup comes early when the 300-plus-member band makes its 7 a.m. rounds through campus, a "let's get ready to rumble" march that targets the school's many dormitories.

Waking students are greeted by a campus that already has sprung to life. By midmorning, the parking lot south of Notre Dame Stadium is a sea of vehicles and barbecue grills, each contributing its own special aroma to the air of excitement. As dorm chefs fire up their grills, alumni swarm through the bookstore, gather around the Basilica to greet Irish players after their game-day Mass and skip from quad to quad, in search of memories from season's past.

The Notre Dame experience is generational, passed through families like precious heirlooms. And no university has a more national flavor, thanks to an exclusive every-game television contract with NBC and the passionate bond it maintains with former students. Notre Dame games attract alumni from far and wide, many of whom fly into Chicago, Indianapolis or Fort Wayne for a rush hour-like Saturday morning drive to football heaven.

If they're fortunate, they will get to South Bend in time for a lively pregame band concert that attracts thousands of fans, young and old, to the steps of Bond Hall 90 minutes before kickoff. A big part of that show is the 10-person Irish Guard, an elite group of skilled marchers who clear the way for the band on campus treks and perform special step maneuvers and formations. Scowling, silent and formidable at 6-foot-2 or taller, a Guardsman dresses in a plaid Irish kilt and towers more than 8 feet high when wearing the traditional bearskin shaka.

For half an hour, the Guard stands sentry as the band fires up the crowd, ending the show with an emotion-tugging rendition (come on now, everybody sing) of the Alma Mater. After a 20-minute drum show, the Guard leads the band in a lively march to the Stadium, fans following in a Pied Piper-like trance. It won't take long for that trance to turn into frenzy.

The tunnel is an important piece of Irish tradition. Physically, it connects the north end zone to the locker-room area below the stands. Emotionally, it connects the fans to the players and the struggle they are about to undertake.

In the important 20 or so minutes before every game, this end-zone passageway will become the center of Notre Dame's football universe. First a high-stepping drum major will emerge from the darkness with a dramatic burst, followed by the Irish Guard and the crowd-revving band. Then 80,000 fans will brace for an even more emotional arrival.

One of Notre Dame's best-known traditions has seldom been witnessed in person by fans or media. On the wall, down the first flight of stairs that connects the locker rooms to the tunnel, is a simple gold sign with blue letters that say, "Play Like a Champion Today." One by one, every Irish player files down the stairs, touches the sign for good luck and thus crosses the mental threshold that separates citizen from warrior. The team, emotionally charged, gathers in the tunnel.

The sight of that first golden helmet triggers an explosion that would measure on any Richter scale. It is followed by a sea of glistening gold, fresh paint from the night before, that further charges an already electric atmosphere. Now everybody's ready to rumble and the sellout crowd (the Irish had filled the stadium for 203 of 204 games entering the 2001 season) takes cue from the fired-up blue-and-gold clad Fighting Irish players, who literally jump up and down with anticipation.

From the opening kickoff, nobody in the student

The Irish Guard, a kilt-clad unit that included its first female (below) in 2000, leads the band on its marches and becomes part of the game-day atmosphere.

Before rising to stardom in pro football, Joe Montana (above) won accolades as a quarterback at Notre Dame.

section (from the northwest end zone to the 50-yard line) sits. This is the crazy area, where the noise level seldom dips and such activities as body surfing and referee baiting are both tolerated and encouraged. The cheerleaders know where the action is and stay close to the students, who react passionately to every play and count off the leprechaun mascot's "air pushups" after every score. The band works the crowd from its sideline perch opposite the students in the corner of the north end zone.

One of the highlights between the third and fourth quarters is a special cheer, recited to the music of the 1812 Overture with hand gestures tailored as a tribute to the current head coach. A more curious highlight of the fourth quarter is the anti-drunk-driving message delivered by Sergeant Tim McCarthy, a member of the Indiana State Police. When McCarthy is introduced over the speakers, the stadium grows eerily silent—so quiet you can hear a flask drop. Then McCarthy delivers his message, usually in the form of a bad pun ("Those who have one for the road may have a policeman as a chaser") and the fans explode with touchdown-caliber fury. But one of the most endearing traditions is saved for the end.

Win or lose, the band plays the fight song one more time as the players file over to the student section and lift their helmets forward in a salute to the fans. Then, after the team has left the field, the band strikes up one more rendition of the Alma Mater as fans lock shoulders, sway back and forth and sing—an out-of-tune but heartfelt tribute to what so many, from coast to coast and beyond, have come to respect.

That special, hard-to-deny, in-your-face Notre Dame tradition.

Former coaches Knute Rockne (left) and Frank Leahy, like the legendary Four Horsemen (right), are part of Notre Dame's rich football heritage.

Few football atmospheres can rival the one at Notre Dame, especially when the Irish 'play like a champion.'

Every Saturday in Autumn · Texas A&M Aggies

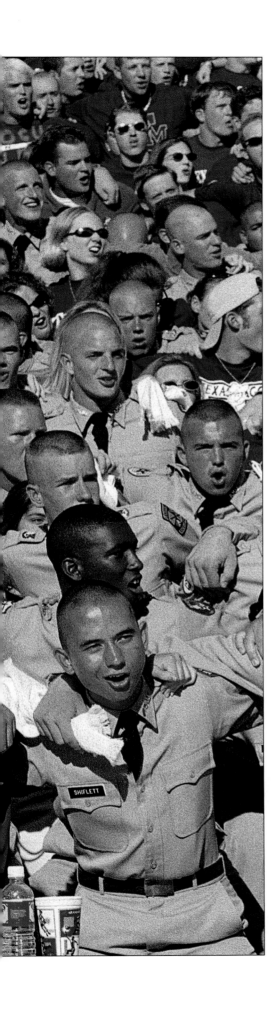

TEXAS A&M
UNIVERSITY

AGGIES

They're loud, proud and fearless, serious-minded traditionalists who answer their critics with a heartfelt "aaaaaaaaaaaay" or an emotional "whoop!" Go ahead, crack a joke or laugh derisively at their expense, but understand you're poking fun at future movers and shakers, patrons of the arts, military heroes and distinguished people of vision. They drive you crazy with their over-the-edge fervor but win your heart with unwavering dedication to such principles as honor and loyalty.

When you visit the east Texas football oasis of College Station on a fall weekend, beware the Aggies. They're everywhere, and they're sure to immerse you in their gospel of rural and military tradition. You might look with amusement at their obsessions, but you can't help but admire their unflagging enthusiasm. From the moment you set foot on the sprawling campus of Texas A&M, you're in for a slightly off-kilter sample of one of the craziest college football atmospheres ever conceived.

Football, Texas style, with an "Ay, Ay, Ay, Whoop!"

To get a feel for A&M, you start with the Corps of Cadets. The Corps relishes and promotes its unofficial title as "Keepers of the Tradition" and there is plenty to keep at this onetime all-male military school. The Corps, a now-voluntary organization that numbers 2,100 members out of a huge student population of 44,000, remains front and center in campus life, actively promotes student unity and jumps forward at every opportunity to keep Aggie brethren aware of the school's rich military heritage.

The Corps' influence is hard to miss. Cadets make up the entire 400-plus-member Aggie band, one of the top precision marching units in the country. They organize and execute such important traditions as Silver Taps and Muster, emotional ceremonies that honor Aggies and former Aggies who have died. They also participate in community service projects, actively par-

Kyle Field, a three-sided monster, can give opponents a claustrophobic sense of helplessness.

ticipate in student government and work endlessly to promote the "Spirit of Aggieland." One of the most "spirited" traditions organized by the Corps has been a massive bonfire built by the student body before every game against hated rival Texas.

The Corps also maintains visibility through Reveille VII, an American Collie that serves as the school's official mascot. The very serious responsibility of caring for Reveille falls to Company E-2

and a sophomore corporal who enjoys the honor of escorting the "First Lady of A&M" around campus (even to class) and tending to her needs. Whenever Reveille VII, the highest-ranking member of the Corps, crosses paths with a freshman Cadet (or Fish), he is required to address her, "Howdy, Miss Reveille, Ma'am"—failure of which is considered a serious breach of conduct.

To illustrate Texas A&M's dedication to tradition, consider this: Reveille dates back to 1931, when a stray puppy was adopted by the Corps and became an active participant in all Cadet activities. For years, the first four Reveilles were buried in the north end of Kyle Field, an open area that allowed them full view of the scoreboard during football games. When a late-1990s stadium renovation added three levels to the north end zone and forced removal of the Reveille graves to a nearby park, a Cadet was stationed out-

side the stadium during games, armed with a transistor radio and dry erase board that he updated and held aloft in front of the graves every time the score changed.

After construction was completed in 1999, the Reveilles were exhumed again and reburied outside the stadium's north entrance in Twelfth Man Plaza. They were joined by Reveille V, who died and was given a military-style memorial service that attracted more than 3,000 mourners to Kyle Field. Now all the former Reveilles have an unfettered view of an electric scoreboard—

Signs on high-rising facades, a packed house and the Aggie Band are fall Saturday staples at A&M.

First call for football comes when the Aggie Band leads a full complement of Cadets down Houston Street to Kyle Field.

facing their graves on the exterior of the stadium.

Aggies know how to yell. They should because they get plenty of practice. Before they officially set foot on campus, before they ever attend their first class or purchase their first book, they are instructed on the fine art of delivering maximum vocal support to the cause at hand.

An Aggie never cheers. He yells, always while "humping it"— bent at the waist with hands placed just above the knees; back, mouth and throat properly aligned for maximum volume. A&M does not have cheerleaders; it has yell leaders, three seniors and two juniors who are elected by the student body and usually become campus celebrities. There is no jumping, somersaulting or other creative maneuvers to inspire A&M fans. The goal at A&M is "loud," and everyone participates enthusiastically in yells that have been passed through the school for generations.

The yell is part of A&M's storied Twelfth Man tradition. As the story goes, E. King Gill, a basketball player who played briefly on the football team, was watching from the press box in January 1922 when A&M played Centre College in a postseason game at Dallas. As Aggie after Aggie left the game because of injury, coach Dana X. Bible sent word that he needed Gill to come down and suit up. Gill responded, donning the uniform of an injured player, but he never had to go into the game.

A member of the Corps' cavalry unit puts the final game-day touches on his mount.

Gill's heroic gesture will never be forgotten. A statue of Gill, the original Twelfth Man, stands outside the north entrance to Kyle Field. But the real Twelfth Man tradition is carried on by A&M students, who stand throughout every game, ready, like Gill, to jump into the fray. Offshoots of the tradition include the Twelfth Man towels, which are waved vigorously during every game, and the walk-on player (wearing No. 12) who performs every week on the kickoff coverage unit. When 5-foot-9 Twelfth Man Robert Jordan got his chance and made the tackle on the opening kickoff in A&M's 2000 game against Kansas State, Kyle Stadium endured a volcano-like eruption.

Intensity is the name of the game at Texas A&M, from the gyrations of yell leaders (left) to the body English of players and coaches.

While the typical yell might fall short of eruption status during A&M games, it does rank high on any noise meter. "The yells, when done in unison, are loud, really impressive," says former Cadet Simon Gonzalez. "They send chills up and down your spine the first time you hear them. They can be powerful."

The power of the yell is learned early, when all incoming freshmen take part in late-summer "Fish Camp"—a three- or four-day school orientation during which they learn, among other things, the stories behind the many traditions, all the important school-related songs and how to behave at football games. They also have to memorize the yells, which they demonstrate at their first official yell practice (with leaders and partial band) late in orientation.

It all adds up to trouble for opposing football teams, who can find the well-choreographed atmosphere at Kyle Field unsettling and intimidating. Rice coach Ken Hatfield calls Kyle Field "the toughest place I've had to coach." A&M coach R.C. Slocum calls it "a bigtime atmosphere ... something very special." With a 12-year home record of 64-7-1 after the 2000 season, his feelings are understandable.

The massive bonfire, a longtime tradition before every game against Texas, was discontinued for two years after a 1999 accident in which a 40-foot stack of logs collapsed, killing 12 and injuring 27 others. Construction of the bonfire is scheduled to resume in 2002 under more stringent supervision and guidelines.

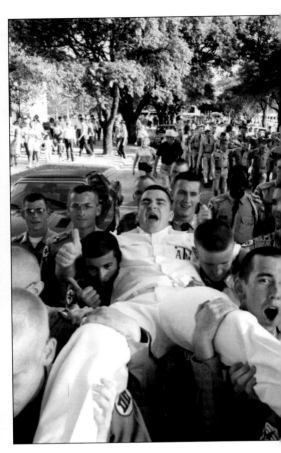

The life of a yell leader is never dull, whether plotting strategy (left) or getting the traditional postgame victory ride to the Pond.

The alumni begin arriving from Houston, San Antonio, Dallas and other strategic points on the overheated Texas map on Friday afternoon, most toting their tailgating equipment and other accessories of comfort. But barbecues will never be the primary focus on a Texas A&M football weekend that officially kicks off with the much-anticipated Friday midnight yell practice.

The fun starts when the Aggie Band forms at the Quadrangle near the Corps dorm and marches, led by torch-carrying yell leaders, to Kyle Field. Fans line the route, fall in behind the parade and file into the east stands (the student side) of the stadium.

Aggies know how to yell. They should because they get plenty of practice.

A typical yell practice will draw 30,000 fans (the 2000 pre-Oklahoma practice pulled in 35,000), ranging from already-partying students to grandmothers and children who prepare for the midnight event with afternoon naps. Over the next hour or so, the fans will practice their yells, sing the War Hymn (A&M's fight song) and Spirit of Aggieland (the Alma Mater) and be regaled by inspirational stories from the theatrically inclined yell leaders. Yell practice festivities end with "lights out," a signal for students to kiss their dates—as they will the next day after every Aggie score.

Game day starts early for the band, which rolls out for a 6 a.m. practice. Visitors, fueled by the aroma of well-stocked barbecue grills, spend most of the morning revisiting memories, which are supplemented with visits to the bookstore, to former dorms and memorial statues honoring former A&M military heroes. One of the most popular stops is the George Bush Presidential Library and Museum, which houses the papers and memorabilia of the 41st President of the United States. It is located on the West Campus, about a mile and a half from Kyle Field down George Bush Drive.

First call for football comes an hour before kickoff, when the Aggie Band leads the full complement of Cadets in a military-style parade down Houston Street to Kyle Field. The band enters the southeast gate, goes into formation, and the rest of the Corps follows in a full-review march around the north end zone. The marchers pass the west-side reviewing stand, where they salute the Commandant of Cadets, his staff and any visiting dignitaries before exiting the southwest gate. Cadets then scatter and re-enter the stadium with tickets.

First-time A&M opponents can be shaken by the overpowering aura of Kyle Field, an 80,650-seat concrete monster. Triple-deck stands rise sharply off both sidelines, and another three-layered section (the Zone) towers above the north end zone, providing an almost claustrophobic sense of helplessness. A sign on the facade between the first and second deck of the student side proclaims this "Home of the 12th Man," and another between the second and third says "Welcome to Aggieland," but any feelings of conviviality are short-lived.

No victory is complete until the yell leaders have been thrown into the Fish Pond, where the real victory celebration begins.

Soon the white-clad leaders are signaling a yell to first-row students, who pass it back with long-practiced efficiency, and the roar cascades throughout the stadium like thunder—every word performed by every voice, 30,000 humping students and 50,000 humping alumni (the sit-downs), in ominous unison. The yells come periodically throughout the game, performed at strategic moments by a very knowledgeable football crowd, and Kyle Field rocks after the first and third quarters when everybody sings and sways to the War Hymn.

Reveille (above) is the 'First Lady of A&M' and one of the most revered mascots in college football. The Aggie Band (below) brings a military flavor to football and other facets of campus life.

Every yell is punctuated by wildcatting, those "Ays" and "Whoops" delivered by students in accordance with class-level privilege. And touchdowns and field goals are punctuated by a single shot from a cannon, positioned in the south end zone area and attended by Cadets from the Corps' mounted cavalry unit, as well as the traditional after-score kiss.

One of the highlights of any game is the halftime show staged by the Aggie Band, which performs a no-nonsense, motivational march program highlighted by straight rows, complex formations and precision moves. The saying around A&M is that the Aggies have "never lost a halftime," and that is confirmed by the way fans remain in the stands for the intermission and explode when the band closes with the traditional "Block T" formation.

The game ends with typical A&M embellishment. The Aggies never lose—they are just outscored, probably because the students didn't yell loud enough. And when that occasionally happens, the students remain in the stands and take part in another yell practice to get ready for the next game.

After a victory, the maroon-clad team will face the student section and join in singing the War Hymn before the freshman Cadets chase down the yell leaders, carry them across campus and throw them into the Fish Pond near Sbisa Hall. Tired and wet, the leaders emerge from the water to conduct—what else?—an impromptu yell practice.

All, of course, in the Spirit of Aggieland.

Jubilation at Kyle Field extends from the sideline all the way to the upper reaches of the triple-tiered facility.

Every Saturday in Autumn · LSU Tigers

LOUISIANA STATE

UNIVERSITY

T I G E R S

By Louisiana standards, it's the total experience—colorful, friendly and distinctively delicious by day, head-spinning, equilibrium-testing, in-your-face crazy by night. It's football with a Cajun accent, 60 minutes of bedlam wrapped in a blanket of Southern hospitality. For college football at its emotional peak, there is no place like Baton Rouge on a typical autumn Saturday.

That Southern hospitality, framed by moss-covered oak trees, fragrant honeysuckles and distinctive architecture, is a way of life on the Louisiana State University campus. The football bedlam is a genetic right of passage, measured by a passion for LSU success and the sound and fury Tiger fans sustain with an almost mythical intensity.

Few venues in sports can match the loud, raucous atmosphere of Tiger Stadium, where excitement hangs over the field like a bayou fog and ear plugs, if not mandatory, come highly recommended. This is a place where opponents can be intimidated, the Tigers can be inspired and even the fans finish the night emotionally drained and physically exhausted.

"Unbelievable, crazy!" said former Southern Cal All-American guard Brad Budde after his first visit to Tiger Stadium in 1979. "That place makes Notre Dame look like Romper Room."

This is a place where opponents can be intimidated, the Tigers can be inspired and even the fans finish the night emotionally drained and physically exhausted.

It's not so much that Louisianans are more boisterous than football fans at other Division I-A schools. It's just that they come to games better prepared. LSU's all-day tailgating parties, enlivened by the most sophisticated combinations of food and drink ever conceived, are as legendary as its tradition of night football, which gives fans more time to shed their inhibitions.

A fall weekend at LSU offers a Mardi Gras-like atmosphere flavored by the pungent smells of Cajun cooking, the soulful strains of Cajun and zydeco music and endless talk about Tigers football—a deep-rooted devotion that literally dictates southern Louisiana lifestyle for four months of every year. LSU fans don't just talk about football, they dis-

The secret of LSU's mystique is in the Cajun cuisine and the desire to out-cook and outdo everybody else in a tailgate extravaganza.

Before every game, LSU fans line the streets to greet Tigers players on their triumphant walk to the stadium.

cuss, analyze and dissect personnel and strategies like coaches do opponents when breaking down film.

Football is the lifeline that connects summer to winter, work to play and generation to generation in this deeply passionate community. After more than four decades, Tiger fans still talk with reverence about the Chinese Bandits, a defensive unit that helped LSU win the 1958 national championship, and describe with unflagging enthusiasm how Billy Cannon ran 89 yards with a punt return that sparked a 7-3 victory over Ole Miss on an incredible Halloween night in 1959.

They care about their legends. They're that important.

So is virtually everything else about LSU football, a point driven home by the sight of more than 50,000 out-of-towners flooding onto campus on Friday and Saturday to join 34,000 students and thou-

More than four decades later, Billy Cannon's 89-yard punt return against Ole Miss (left) remains a source of LSU pride.

sands of Baton Rouge locals in a logistical battle of time versus space. Somehow it all works.

That's because LSU fans, by day, are friendly and warm, quick to share and offer friends and strangers a sample of their special cuisine. And by night, they're united in their vocal and tunnel-vision support of the Tigers.

You have to admire their ingenuity and ability to balance the extremes. Over-the-edge frenzy is a big leap from Southern hospitality.

The LSU campus, spread across 2,000 acres just east of the Mississippi River in southern Baton Rouge, enchants first-time visitors with its rustic charm. Once isolated, the campus now integrates comfortably with a city that has grown to its borders. At first glance, this is no place to go for a good time.

But then Saturday morning fever takes hold. Before the last of the Friday night revelers have begrudgingly answered their wakeup calls, the

campus will have magically transformed into a carnival of food, music and interesting people. The football buzz will be unmistakable; the atmosphere will be electric. For those people looking for something to do, broadcaster Jim Hawthorne, the longtime "Voice of the Tigers," has a simple suggestion.

"The best thing to do on a football Saturday is to walk the campus, check out the people, listen to the music and savor the smell of the incredible food that's being cooked," Hawthorne says. "Just soak up the atmosphere. The people are incredibly friendly and eager to share—and everyone gets to campus early."

The smells are, indeed, incredible. If the crawfish doesn't pull you in, maybe the boiled shrimp or gumbo will. The jambalaya is always tasty, but sometimes you get lucky with boudin noir, creatively prepared deer meat or everybody's favorite, alligator sausage. On a special day, you might be invited to sample the cochon-de-lait (roast pig) being prepared by an adventurous soul on the other side of the parking lot.

Tiger Stadium, big, loud and proud, is at its festive best during pregame.

Tailgating, Louisiana style, is all about everybody trying to outdo and outcook everybody else. The food is served to a backdrop of music, some provided by Cajun and zydeco bands and the more traditional fare by expensive sound systems that have become standard tailgating equipment at LSU. Much of the festive activity takes place around the motor homes and recreational vehicles in the expansive parking lots that fan out from Tiger Stadium, but few nooks and crannies escape use in any section of the campus.

Tailgating is so popular that LSU officials estimate as many as 15,000 fans show up without tickets, content to watch the game on a television somewhere outside the stadium. By 7 p.m., when a typical night game begins, Tigers fans will be stuffed with food, feeling oh-so-good and ready to rumble—a natural extension of their free-wheeling personalities.

On those occasional Saturdays when the Tigers play in the afternoon to satisfy a television commitment, LSU officials brace for a barrage of fan complaints. This, after all, is a serious breach of decorum. Fans will never give up those extra six hours of tailgating without a fight.

Tailgates (below) and fan frenzy (above) are two staples of every LSU football weekend.

LSU fans call him Mike and he lives in a $220,000 home about 200 yards from the stadium, just across North Stadium Drive. He normally leads a quiet life, secure in such outdoor amenities as a pool and climbing platform and free to move indoors to escape inclement weather. He handles his campus celebrity with easy aplomb.

Everything changes for Mike on those crazy fall Saturdays. Thousands of people flock by to get a look at the full-grown Bengal tiger, which ranks among the most heralded mascots in college football. Then it really gets crazy. In late afternoon, Mike is loaded into a special cage and wheeled inside the gate at the southeast entrance of the stadium, where he remains like a sentry guarding the opposing team's locker room.

Imagine the looks Mike gets as those players file past his cage! Then imagine the reaction of LSU fans when Mike's cage, with a dozen or so cheerleaders riding on top, is pulled around the perimeter of the field about a half hour before every game. When the cage stops at the north end by the student section and Mike lets out a mighty growl into an open microphone, the partially filled stadium rocks for the first of many times over the course of a three-hour game.

Mike V (he's the fifth in a line of Bengal Tiger mascots) is just one of several traditions that add to the aura of LSU football. About two hours before game time, LSU players, who have been secluded overnight in a Baton Rouge hotel, are bused to Broussard Hall, where they begin their triumphant walk to the stadium through a corridor of flag-waving, encouragement-yelling fans. An hour later, the Golden Band From Tigerland leaves the Band Hall and marches down North Stadium Drive to the crowd-pleasing strains of "Hold That Tiger"—a song that will become ingrained in the memory of annoyed visitors before the night is over.

The purple-and-gold clad crowd, the traditional home white jerseys, Tiger Paws and painted faces, the tailgating fervor that carries right up to game time and the setting sun, letting everybody know that showtime is only minutes away, add to the colorful atmosphere that makes any self-respecting Tigers fan beam with pride.

It's a big, round, concrete bowl, set strategically on the fringe of football heaven. The first things you notice are the powerful aura, a sense that great things have been accomplished here, and the smells—of hot dogs, stale popcorn, sweat-soaked seats and spilled alcohol, long absorbed into the cracks, crevices and very fibers of an aging structure.

There's nothing frilly about Tiger Stadium, a huge 91,000-seat facility that once doubled as a dormitory for 1,500 students. This is one of the oldest football palaces in the Southeastern Conference (opened in 1924) and it lives up to its considerable mystique and reputation as a "Death Valley" for opposing teams. The double-

Mike the Tiger makes his dramatic pregame entrance (above), much to the delight of always creative LSU fans (below).

decked stands rise quickly on both sidelines and fans almost hang over the action below. The single-decked end zone areas help hold in the sometimes-oppressive heat and the noise that LSU fans are so famous for making.

They like to think of it as pandemonium—a sustained fervor that is so loud it practically lifts you out of your seat. A full day of tailgating, combined with that incredible passion for Tigers football, gives the crowd an extra energy you don't find at other venues. LSU fans consider themselves participants, not viewers, and the noise they create hovers like a thick blanket.

LSU officials still recall the night of October 8, 1988, when quarterback Tommy Hodson beat Auburn with a game-winning touchdown pass to Eddie Fuller and the crowd explosion was so loud that it registered on a seismograph meter at the school's geology department. Legend has it that Cannon's run in 1959 touched off an eruption that so startled Baton Rouge people they ran out of their house to see what was the matter. The bedlam at the end of a 1997 upset victory over No. 1-ranked Florida was a high-light-film staple for months to come.

Tigers are everywhere on game day at LSU—one real, one costumed and many in white, purple and gold football uniforms.

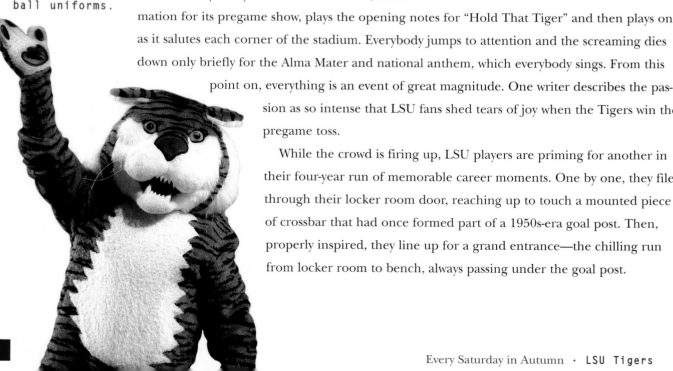

The frenzy really starts when the band, in formation for its pregame show, plays the opening notes for "Hold That Tiger" and then plays on as it salutes each corner of the stadium. Everybody jumps to attention and the screaming dies down only briefly for the Alma Mater and national anthem, which everybody sings. From this point on, everything is an event of great magnitude. One writer describes the passion as so intense that LSU fans shed tears of joy when the Tigers win the pregame toss.

While the crowd is firing up, LSU players are priming for another in their four-year run of memorable career moments. One by one, they file through their locker room door, reaching up to touch a mounted piece of crossbar that had once formed part of a 1950s-era goal post. Then, properly inspired, they line up for a grand entrance—the chilling run from locker room to bench, always passing under the goal post.

4

Everybody in the stadium is jumping, including the players.

And so it goes. The night is filled with a loud, steady buzz that seldom fades and is interrupted by periodic crowd eruptions and occasional groans. The cheerleaders are active, whether inciting the students to even greater volume or bowing in reverence after an LSU touchdown. Bodies are passed around the stands, everybody dances and sings to "Tiger Rag" and the fight song and when LSU scores, there are hugs and kisses all around.

Winning only increases the volume and emotion, something the Tigers had trouble accomplishing with any consistency from 1989-94 under coaches Mike Archer and Curley Hallman. The pain of that era was intense, but no more so than the ecstasy of every LSU win.

At game's end, the party atmosphere picks up where it left off. Hang around long enough and the players might even show up, hoping to get some food and a few pats on the back. The exodus is not complete until Sunday morning or afternoon, at which time Baton Rouge returns, temporarily at least, to a reasonable level of sanity.

Sunset at Tiger Stadium is a beautiful prelude to one of LSU's more valued traditions: night football.

Every Saturday in Autumn · Nebraska Cornhuskers

THE UNIVERSITY OF
NEBRASKA

CORNHUSKERS

They swarm into town from every direction, red-covered fanatics from such Nebraska football strongholds as Scottsbluff, Ogallala, McCook, Valentine, Beatrice and Wahoo. It's a fall Saturday ritual, like swallows returning to their own special Capistrano. Soon the farmers, laborers and ranchers of America's heartland will be cheering and celebrating alongside its bankers, lawyers and doctors.

Such is the unifying power of Nebraska football that loyalty to the Big Red transcends time, class and gender—a statewide devotion no other major university can match. Check out any Nebraska city during a Cornhuskers game. Flags and banners will be everywhere, streets will be empty and patrons at those stores, restaurants and bars that are open will be huddled around a radio or television.

In Lincoln, the capital of Nebraska in more ways than one, everything will be hopping. Life is good for those lucky enough to have football tickets, and the thousands who don't will simply

Nebraska fans, with colorful zest, turn Memorial Stadium into an eye-straining sea of red on football Saturdays.

bask in the revved-up atmosphere of big-time college football. Excitement rolls through the city like a giant wave before eventually engulfing and overflowing 74,031-seat Memorial Stadium, where every game has been sold out for almost four decades.

Call it passion, call it fanaticism, call it over the edge. Nebraska fans will travel anywhere to watch their Cornhuskers—and they feel like they're part of the team. It's an ownership thing, a kinship and sense of family that helps sustain and energize one of the most successful programs in the country.

To appreciate a fall weekend in Lincoln, you first must understand the deep feelings most Nebraskans have for the Cornhuskers. This is not an infatuation. College football, with no major professional sports to steal its spotlight, has been the center of the state's universe for a century, a pride that has been passed down through generations like a precious family heirloom.

Over an amazing 36-year period, Bob Devaney (left) and Tom Osborne guided Nebraska to 356 wins and five national championships.

Parents dream about sending their children to Nebraska, just as their parents had entertained hopes for them. Those lucky parents with an athletic son relish the idea of him someday stepping onto the Memorial Stadium field wearing red and white, a future Johnny Rodgers, Dave Rimington, Mike Rozier, Dean Steinkuhler, or Tommie Frazier. The virtues of Nebraska football are so deeply ingrained in state athletes that many, capable of securing full scholarships at other universities, choose to pay their own way as walk-ons and gamble that, eventually, they will be able to win a roster spot. Many do.

The Cornhuskers' depth-sustaining walk-on program has gained national renown and played a major role in one of the most amazing success stories in sports history. In the 36-year span

Everything is chaotic when the Cornhuskers, led by coach Frank Solich, run out of the tunnel to get ready for the opening kickoff.

from 1962, when Bob Devaney began his 11-year reign as coach, through 1997, when Tom Osborne ended his 25-year tenure, Nebraska won five national championships and 356 games, led the nation in winning percentage, captured 21 Big Eight and Big 12 conference titles, appeared in 34 bowl games, finished in the nation's Top 10 28 times and produced 26 first-round NFL draft picks and 64 All-Americans.

When Osborne retired after winning his third national title in 1997, Frank Solich stepped in and won 31 of his first 38 games. But Osborne did not just disappear. He threw his hat into the political arena in 2000 and was elected to Congress out of Nebraska's third district with a whopping 83 percent of the popular vote, soundly defeating Rollie Reynolds, a huge Cornhuskers football fan.

Such is life that after the 2000 season, Nebraskans had witnessed 39 consecutive winning campaigns and watched their Cornhuskers make 32 straight bowl appearances. But don't confuse supreme confidence with arrogance. These are fans who will greet visitors with a smile, welcome them with open arms to their tailgate party and show respect to opponents, who can count on getting a standing ovation after each game. These are players who, after three hours of battering and getting battered, will invite their enemies to share a postgame prayer with them at midfield.

Cornhuskers are easy to spot, from their red clothing to other identifying features.

It's all part of the Nebraska way. Cornhuskers shred opponents with machine-like efficiency and send them away with warm and fuzzy memories.

At first glance, Memorial Stadium is a startling deviation from the flat, featureless prairie that dominates one of the biggest agricultural states in the union. It is big and powerful, a hulking monument that challenges Lincoln's Capitol building for local distinction. It also is the centerpiece for Huskermania, a not-so-subtle sense of anticipation that explodes into frenzy on football weekends.

It's everywhere. Just stroll around the spread-out Nebraska campus or the adjoining streets of downtown Lincoln and you're bombarded by everything Husker—a quick lesson of how closely business and life are tied to football in this city. Lincoln literally turns red when the Cornhuskers are in town, and everybody wants a piece of the action.

You will get the idea if you check out O Street in downtown Lincoln on a Friday

night. That's where a majority of Nebraska's 25,000 students will be—eating, drinking and feeding their football fever at nightclubs and restaurants along the strip. You'll find everything from sidewalk bars to raucous theme establishments like the Sidetrack Lounge, where patrons have been Husking down the corny, homemade songs of Joyce Durand for almost a quarter century.

Football is definitely on display five miles or so away at Misty's, where Friday night patrons rub shoulders with members of the Cornhusker Marching Band and Nebraska cheerleaders. Many fans will head for Barry's, P.O. Pears and the Embassy Suites on Saturday for organized tailgating within easy walking distance of Memorial Stadium.

Huskermania is not a life-long passion—it goes well beyond that.

But the best place to experience Huskermania is on a spread-out campus that fans out to the east of the stadium. Parking lots are filled with creative tailgaters, excited chatter fills the air and the pleasant smell of Huskerburgers and Huskerdogs on the grill is enhanced by a cacophony of sounds that gives the place a carnival-like feel.

Kids are throwing footballs, music is blaring and broadcaster-like voices espouse the merits

Memorial Stadium has its peaceful side, but never on football Saturdays.

of Nebraska football on the pregame show and highlight tapes. Televisions with portable satellite dishes are tuned in to other games. Everywhere you look, friendly fans are mingling, talking football and inviting strangers to share their food.

If you're looking for the more elaborate spreads, walk over to Lot 12, directly east of the stadium. If you're interested in a more lively experience, go to the Nebraska Union where students will be throwing their own special tailgate party. Rest assured that wherever you end up, the atmosphere will be electric.

The best bet for any visitor might be to walk the campus, soak up the festive atmosphere and check out such buildings as Morrill Hall, the Beadle Center, Sheldon Gallery and the 30,000-square-foot strength training facility, one of the most advanced and celebrated weight complexes in the nation.

> **If you've never seen Memorial Stadium at its fan-bulging best, you're in for a treat. The stands are an eye-straining, solid mass of red ... 75,000-plus fans in full battle gear.**

If you've never seen Memorial Stadium at its fan-bulging best, you're in for a treat. The stands are an eye-straining, solid mass of red, from top to bottom of both double-decked sides and both single-level end zones—75,000-plus fans in full battle gear.

That mesmerizing passion does not seem out of line at one of the grandest facilities in all of football. Opened in 1923 and expanded over the years from its original 31,000 capacity, Memorial Stadium combines an old-time ambience with the wonders of modern technology. The ancient ramps and corridors still retain their

traditional feel; the corner towers, the turrets with American and Nebraska flags flying from their top, still bear inscriptions ("Their lives they held the country's trust; they kept its faith; they died its heroes") honoring Nebraskans who have died in wars.

But now the once single-tiered west stands tower over the field—two decks topped by a press-box and luxurious skyboxes that allow fans to view a friendly Lincoln skyline to the southeast. Two state-of-the-art HuskerVision screens have opened up a whole new world to fans who take special pride in their tradition.

The screens play a prominent role in the most poignant moment of any Nebraska game: the famed Tunnel Walk. This is a choreographed opening act that fans arrive early to catch—a communication of such themes as tradition, success and family.

The pregame always begins with the Cornhusker Band, which performs a short, traditional show that concludes with a march to the south stadium tunnel, where a human corridor is formed. Once the band is in place, the HuskerVision screens go black—no sound system, no music, no images of any kind. So it remains for the next minute or more, an almost eerie calm

The Marching Red (above) and Lil' Red (below), the Cornhuskers' inflatable mascot, keep things lively with a variety of well-chore-ographed side-line routines.

that prompts the restless crowd to begin a rhythmic clap. At the first sound from a suddenly recharged speaker, the crowd erupts.

All eyes shift to the two screens, which begin a computer-animated presentation that changes from year to year. National championships have been a popular theme in recent times. Other themes can be general or specific to great players and memories from the past.

The presentation in the 2000 season went something like

Nebraska is a tough place to play, in equal parts because of the Big Red passion that engulfs the stadium and the team's winning reputation.

this: A football appears on the screen, seemingly from outer space. It flies by the skyboxes and over the Capitol building. "The Sower," a 19-foot bronze figure that stands atop the Capitol with his bag of seed, suddenly turns and strikes the Heisman Trophy pose. He grabs the football and throws it toward Memorial Stadium, six blocks away. It sails inside, strikes a helmet representing the opposing team near midfield and explodes, as does the crowd.

At this point, the screen switches to a live camera just outside the Nebraska locker room under the south stands. The team, revved up and excited after receiving its final pep talk, walks out the door and down the tunnel. As the progression makes its way toward the field entrance, the players hear the roaring crowd and become even more excited. By the time they run out of the tunnel and through the band, everything is chaotic.

And so it will remain.

Nebraskans take pride in their Midwest values. They don't have the hard-edged, in-your-face mentality associated with many major programs, but don't let that fool you. Despite the respectful greeting, despite the warm after-game ovations, Memorial Stadium is an intimidating place to play.

The Tunnel Walk has been known to leave opposing players overwhelmed, which is why many coaches choose to keep their teams secluded in the locker room until it's over. But more than anything, the Cornhuskers intimidate by reputation.

Nebraska has won more than 75 percent of its home games in Memorial Stadium's eight-decade history—and that figure is a lot higher since 1962, Devaney's first season. The

5

Cornhuskers have not won fewer than nine games in any season since 1968 and they lost only three home games in the 1990s, a decade in which they won three national championships. In short, winning makes it easier for fans to be respectful.

So does the way Nebraska wins. Most games are like a sustained victory parade, opponents overmatched by halftime or mid-third quarter. Fans get caught up in the celebration, which is like food for their soul. They revel in the antics of Lil' Red, an inflatable mascot that has won national awards, and still enjoy Herbie Husker, the familiar figure in the oversized cowboy hat. They go crazy over the hot dog-dispensing abilities of Der Viener Schlinger, who, according to legend, has shot one over the 100-foot-high skyboxes with his portable bun gun.

The Tunnel Walk has been known to leave opposing players overwhelmed. ... But more than anything, the Cornhuskers intimidate by reputation.

You can always count on the Marching Red to keep things lively with its well-choreographed sideline and halftime routines, and when things really get out of hand, you can count on seeing the wave. It usually starts in the southeast corner, the student section, and works its way around and around the stadium with increasing enthusiasm.

Through it all, Nebraska fans never lose touch with the game. They are loud and intimidating when needed, always mindful of how players are performing and adjustments that need to be made. These are knowledgeable fans who will discuss, analyze, dissect and argue about plays, players and game plans well into the night as their tailgate parties wind down.

Every contest ends with Nebraska players gathering near midfield with interested opponents for a postgame prayer. They hold hands in a circle, thank God for health, success and other considerations and then head for their respective locker rooms.

Many fans remain seated to watch postgame interviews on the HuskerVision screens, secure in the knowledge that life in this football haven is just about as good as it gets.

Win or lose, every Nebraska game ends with a prayer, often with opposing players joining the midfield ritual.

Every Saturday in Autumn · Nebraska Cornhuskers

Every Saturday in Autumn · Florida Gators

THE UNIVERSITY OF
FLORIDA

G A T O R S

There are ways to prepare for a visit to Florida Field, but none come highly recommended. You can spend three hours with a brass band in a telephone booth, swim across an alligator-infested river, outrun the snarling bulls at Pamplona and endure the heat of a fiery blast furnace.

Loud, intimidating, intense and hot— such is life in one of the most dreaded snakepits in college football. And then it gets really unpleasant.

6

Before a typical football Saturday ends in Gainesville, visiting teams will be stomped, chomped and romped by coach Steve Spurrier's scoring machine, one of the sleekest, fastest and most efficient offenses ever unleashed.

The intimidation starts right at the top at the University of Florida, where Ben Hill Griffin Stadium at Florida Field has been given a more earthy nickname. "The Swamp," Spurrier calls it. "The swamp is where Gators live. We feel comfortable there, but we hope our opponents feel tentative. A swamp is hot and sticky and can be dangerous."

"Hot and sticky" is fact; "dangerous" is perception. But the combination of a championship-caliber team, the body-sapping Florida heat and the tunnel-vision intensity of loud, irreverent fans is enough to strike fear in anybody. These fans are proud of their ability to intimidate, and that pride is used as a game-day weapon.

Florida Field is no place for the meek or anybody with a low tolerance for pain—the ear-splitting, head-pounding, heart-throbbing, sweaty, smelly kind of pain that Gators fans provide, always with a heavy dose of good cheer.

They come in droves, football-obsessed fanatics from Jacksonville, Orlando, Tampa-St. Petersburg, Sarasota and smaller cities throughout and beyond the massive Florida peninsula. They are not discreet or subtle, dedicated in dress and demeanor to the Spurrier directives of supporting their Gators and making life miserable for the enemy.

Gators are plentiful at the University of Florida, both the human and animal variety.

On most days of the year, these are real estate brokers, lawyers, mechanics and merchants who forge a living out of the vast tourism trade that fuels Florida's economy. But on football weekends, they close up their businesses, desert the beaches, stretch out their vocal cords and aim their orange-and-blue-decorated vehicles for Gainesville, a classic college community of 88,000 in the north-central portion of the state.

Like nearby Disney World, Busch Gardens, Cape Canaveral, Sea World and the beautiful Atlantic and Gulf coasts, Florida football is a seasonal attraction. But unlike those theme parks and beaches that bring millions of visitors to the Sunshine State, the Gators are a year-long

addiction—a passion that has been passed on through generations of fans.

When Spurrier guided his alma mater to the school's first national championship in 1996, 70,000 of those fans flocked to Florida Field for an emotional victory celebration. The spring game typically draws 35,000 and every Friday night before the annual homecoming game, more than 70,000 show up at The Swamp for what Florida bills as the world's largest student-run pep rally. Gator Growl is an entertainment extravaganza that includes Spurrier and his players, the Pride of the Sunshine band, cheerleaders, student skits and a big-name comedian—performers like Robin Williams, Rodney Dangerfield, Jerry Seinfeld and Bill Cosby.

It's no coincidence that the 1990 arrival of Spurrier, a Heisman Trophy-winning quarterback for the Gators in 1966, coincided with a string of sellouts that stretched to 73 in the 2000 season. Neither is it coincidence that the Gators reached a level of excellence in the decade that few programs ever achieve—a 57-4 record at home, at least nine wins every season and 102 overall,

Palm trees greet visitors to Ben Hill Griffin Stadium, which soon will transform into The Swamp.

Florida fans know how to deal with the heat, whether turning it up on opponents (right) or finding momentary relief (below) during pregame festivities.

five Southeastern Conference titles and 10 or more victories for six straight years (1993-98).

Spurrier's understanding of fan support is almost as sophisticated as his high-powered passing attacks. He plays on emotion, uses images of alligators, swamps and "our home" to get fans fired up and urges them to get even louder if he really wants to distract an opponent. When a football god speaks, these fans always listen.

And it doesn't hurt that Florida boasts one of the biggest student ticket allotments (about 21,000) in the nation. Wild, crazy and intimidating, they are merely another weapon for the coach who already has everything.

It's hot, a broiling oven that cooks thousands of Florida fans into a game-day frenzy. Gainesville smolders helplessly in the middle of the state, a flat, steamy sauna located too far from the coasts to benefit from their gentle sea breezes.

This is no place for the weak of heart, and those who make the journey to Gatorland come well prepared—and in uniform. Gaudy, orange-and-blue combinations of shorts, T-shirts and caps displaying various forms of Florida affiliation are mandatory. So are food, drink, a tailgating umbrella to fight off the sun and, of course, those Florida football essentials—shades and sunscreen.

Oak trees are plentiful on the Florida campus, but more than 80,000 people cannot hide from the noonday sun. So perspiration becomes a badge of honor—an unpleasant accessory on those scorching mid-90s afternoons in September and early October. These are fans who can stand the heat, but even their stamina will be tested before the day is through.

The sun will be only a soft, morning blur

when tailgaters begin setting up on asphalt parking lots and street corners that by midafternoon will have become blistering radiators. Quickly the 2,000-acre, 42,000-student campus transforms into an orange-and-blue festival, a menagerie of music, highlight tapes, pregame radio broadcasts and intricate football discussions that will carry right up to the typical 3:30 kickoff.

Many of the more extravagant spreads can be found in a garage and lot just south of the stadium where some recreational vehicles will have been parked since Thursday. Other tailgaters fill the huge O'Connell Center lot to the west and some even buy space in the front yards of neighborhoods to the north.

Every lot, street corner and open space throughout the campus turns into a maze of grills, tables, lawn chairs, generator-powered fans and food, ranging from the catered meals with table cloths, candles and wine to the more basic chips and a 12-pack. Body-painted fans, creatively decorated cars and full-costumed Gators keep things lively, as does a spirited pregame march by the Pride of the Sunshine band up North-South Drive to the stadium.

The University Avenue strip features such popular hang-outs as the Purple Porpoise and a restaurant called, appropriately, the Swamp (below).

You get a sense that Gainesville is trapped in a festive football vacuum, and the electricity only builds as game time approaches. It even reaches such favorite campus stopoffs as Lake Alice, a picturesque on-campus wildlife sanctuary where live alligators roam; the Bat House, an honest-

This is... THE SWAMP

More than 70,000 fans showed up at The Swamp for the emotional 1996 national championship celebration.

to-goodness home for tens of thousands creatures of the night; and Century Tower, the distinctive campus landmark that chimes out the Alma Mater with its cast-bells carillon.

Ask any Florida student where to go on a football weekend and you'll probably end up at a strip of restaurants, bars and shops near the stadium on University Avenue—a major artery that runs east across campus and eventually hits downtown Gainesville. The University Avenue strip is to Florida Field what Bourbon Street is to the French Quarter.

For Friday night fun, students pack into hotspots like the Purple Porpoise, the Grog House and the Swamp Restaurant, a celebration that lasts far into the morning hours. On game day, the strip becomes shoulder-to-shoulder gridlock, a carnival-like atmosphere of live bands, barbecue tents and organized keg parties. This is where fans work themselves into a "kill the enemy" frenzy and the craziness is only exacerbated by parties at nearby fraternity houses.

Soon all the voices will unite in controlled mayhem and noise will rain over Florida Field in deafening torrents. The Swamp isn't just loud, it's harsh and vindictive. These are admittedly obnoxious fans who take their Gators seriously and demonstrate that loyalty by pummeling opponents with nonstop abuse—like sharks smelling blood in the water.

"I rank Ben Hill Griffin Stadium at Florida Field as the nation's toughest stadium," says ABC analyst and former quarterback Bob Griese. "The Swamp is deafening."

"The Swamp" is an appropriate name. It's hot, muggy and intimidating, like Gators swimming in a lake you have to cross. The bone-chilling theme from Jaws is played over and over and fans respond, all 83,000-plus, by extending their arms up and down in a chomping motion. They also chomp for Nine Inch Nails, a heavy-metal sound that affects some like finger-nails on a chalk board.

If you think that's bad, consider how opposing players and fans must feel with 21,000 revved-up Florida students screaming at them with maniacal enthusiasm. Until the prac-tice was outlawed in 2000, students would leave the stadium at halftime with out-passes, run across the street to the Purple Porpoise and get back for the second half, reinvigorated.

Such is the personality of Florida Field that it grates on opposing fans and players in many ways. This massive facility, built in 1930, dominates the Gainesville landscape, an enclosed red-brick and concrete structure that is guarded at its north end zone entrance by a giant alligator sculpture. There's a sense of intimidation before you even enter.

That feeling intensifies inside. Noise bounces around the stadium like a beach ball, held in by a north end zone that rises to three levels and a double-tiered south end topped by a state-of-the-

Packed Florida Field (below) is like a bad nightmare for Gator oppo-nents, who are lucky to get out with arms and legs still attached.

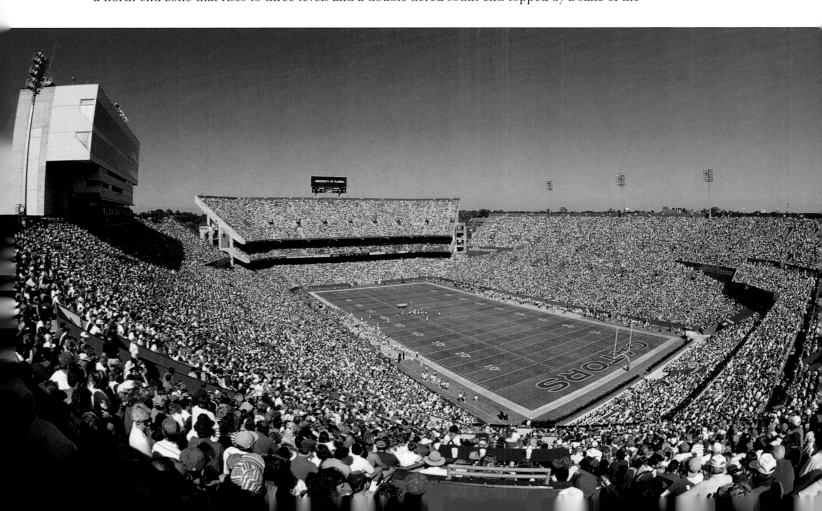

art video board. But The Swamp's most distinctive feature, the one that best defines what this place is all about, is its intimacy. Extremely narrow sidelines create the ominous sensation that Gator fans are right on top of the field, close enough, perhaps, to reach out and touch someone.

Extremely narrow sidelines create the ominous sensation that Gator fans are right on top of the field, close enough, perhaps, to reach out and touch someone.

George Edmondson has been a visible part of Gators football since 1948, a crowd-pleasing superfan dressed in a long-sleeve yellow shirt with orange-and-blue tie, moving from section to section of Florida Field to lead rousing cheers of "Two bits, four bits, six bits, a dollar. ..." Mr. Two-Bits is in semi-retirement now, but he does show up occasionally to participate in one of college football's most colorful pregame introductions.

For special games, the Tampa-based Edmondson will join Mic-Man at midfield after the Florida band has completed its program and formed a corridor at the south end zone players' tunnel. First Mic-Man (a.k.a. Richard Johnston) gets everyone revved up with his "Orange ... Blue" battle of the lungs competition between the east and west stands. Then Mr. Two-Bits works his magic as Jaws music sends the crowd into a chomping fury. All eyes focus on the video board.

The intensity level at Florida is always high, thanks in no small part to fiery Gators coach Steve Spurrier.

Alligators are everywhere, swimming, diving into dark, murky swamp water and lying menacingly on soggy ground. Suddenly a giant gator, facing the screen, opens its mouth wide, wider—ready to devour anything in sight. As the words, "The Swamp. Only Gators get out alive!" flash across the screen, a mighty roar shakes Florida Field and public address announcer Jim Finch bellows, "He-e-e-e-e-e-e-r-e come the Gators."

It's a mind-blowing din as the orange-helmeted, blue-jerseyed players burst onto the field and the noise won't die down until the first play from scrimmage—after an opening kickoff to the music of Nine Inch Nails, complete with more chomping and gnashing of teeth. By halftime, anybody not soaked in sweat probably is somewhere other than Florida Field.

The intensity, like the noise level, remains high throughout the game. The cheerleaders, costumed mascots Albert and Alberta and the band add to an electric atmosphere that is both fun and edgy. One minute The Swamp will rock to the power of "Go Gators," the next it will sway and rejoice to the sound of fans, arms interlocked, singing, "We are the boys from old Florida." That end-of-the-third quarter ritual is both emotional and impressive.

So is a Florida team that seems oblivious to the heat and machine-like in its play until the final gun. Then the players show a softer, gentler side by assembling near midfield to join with fans in the singing of the Alma Mater. When Florida suffered one of its rare home losses in the 1990s, the players quickly left the field, only to be pulled back out by Spurrier. A postgame prayer at midfield typically punctuates the afternoon.

A long, exhausting, exciting and rewarding afternoon that comes with a sustained intensity you don't find at a lot of other college football venues.

George Edmondson (left), Florida's popular Mr. Two-Bits, was a fixture in the stands for many years before going into semi-retirement.

Every Saturday in Autumn · Auburn Tigers

TIGERS

"War Eagle!" The first cry of discovery is delivered with a hungry sense of expectancy as people jump to their feet, turn their heads from side to side and frantically scan the football field below. "War Eagle! War Eagle!" The words grow in frequency and intensity, scattered cries from different parts of a packed stadium. "War Eagle! War Eagle!" The words boom out now in chilling unison, 85,000 voices joined in powerful purpose. "War Eagle!"

There she is, perched proudly on the arm of a handler and apparently oblivious to the storm she has triggered. Suddenly she flies straight to the goalpost, pauses and then lifts off as a collective gasp fills Jordan-Hare Stadium. Soon she's soaring majestically overhead, circling, round and round, homing in on some unseen object below.

"War-r-r-r-r-r-r-r Eagle! War-r-r-r-r-r-r-r-r Eagle!" She dips without warning, arcs and darts forward, a bird of prey preparing to strike. "War-r-r-r-r-r-r-r-r Eagle!" She's a guided missile angling toward the 50-yard line, talons extended with menacing intent. "War-r-r-r-r-r-r-r-r Eagle!" She hits her mark, a perfectly scripted ending to one of the most dramatic beginnings in college football.

The War Eagle has landed. Let the game begin.

Auburn University sneaks up on you, a collection of multi-storied buildings that tower over their rural east-central Alabama surroundings. Metropolitan America this is not, which is just fine with most students and alumni who enjoy the natural intimacy of "the loveliest village in the plains."

Tiger, Auburn's venerable War Eagle, helps keep Jordan-Hare Stadium fans rocking at a fever pitch.

But don't be fooled by Auburn's slow-paced innocence. Hidden beneath its sleepy exterior and down-home charm is a football factory, stoked by a passion that rivals any in the Deep South. On five or six Saturdays every fall, this "village" emerges from its cocoon to become one of the most festive and football-intense communities in all the land.

There's nothing mysterious about this transformation, which is mirrored on fall Saturdays throughout the football-crazy Southeastern Conference. It's all about deep-rooted love, traditions, rivalries, memories, success and passion, cloaked by a social extravaganza that draws thousands of fans from such Alabama and Georgia cities as Birmingham, Montgomery, Dothan, Atlanta and Columbus, all within a 120-mile radius.

Game days would not be the same without Aubie, one of the most beloved costumed mascots in college football.

Auburn is nothing if not traditional. Fans will enchant you with tales of such legendary Tigers as Bo Jackson and Pat Sullivan, touch you emotionally with their Tiger Walk, pound you into submission with their "War Eagle" battle cry, scare you with their utter contempt for the University of Alabama and snow you, visually, with their victory celebrations at Toomer's Corner.

They'll also welcome and feed you during an extensive pregame tailgate party staged with a contagious zest for fun and camaraderie. From Friday evening to Saturday night, an orange-and-blue haze will envelop this community of 38,000, an aromatic delight that suggests something special is cooking. It usually is, from the parking lots that surround Jordan-Hare Stadium on central campus to the cotton fields and farms that border Auburn and its sister city of Opelika.

Just wander the 22,000-student campus and take in the sights and sounds. Roped-off areas and tents suggest corporate or Alumni Association functions, often spiced up by a band. Motor home tailgaters enjoy their satellite-fed televisions, which give them pregame football shows and early-starting telecasts of SEC rivals. The stadium public address system blares music and talk show discussions that can be heard by those nearby. Radio stations set up on-campus remotes and one area near the baseball field even offers interactive fun for the kids.

Everywhere, the atmosphere is electric and the focus is on football. Armchair coaches welcome wanderers and even rival fans, who stop by for food, drink and friendly banter. This is all about forming new friendships, renewing old ones and separating, for a few hours at least, from the rigors of everyday life.

And you quickly get the feeling that Auburn fans are very good at it.

If you're looking for downtown Auburn, walk north on College Street until you hit Magnolia and then get out your microscope. There's really not much to see. Auburn students and fans will tell you that downtown and campus are actually one and the same, a perception that's difficult to argue.

Don't be fooled by Auburn's slow-paced innocence. Hidden beneath its sleepy exterior and down-home charm is a football factory, stoked by a passion that rivals any in the Deep South.

The junction of College and Magnolia is interesting for a more compelling reason. Locals call it Toomer's Corner and it's a very busy area that plays a vital part in any football weekend. If you want to sample the "best lemonade in the land," stop at Toomer's Drug Store—a place once frequented, according to legend, by former Auburn coach John Heisman back in the 1890s. But Heisman, the man for whom the Heisman Trophy was named, was not around many years later when the area became popular for another reason.

Toomer's Corner has long been the gathering place for ecstatic fans after a victory. Thousands will make the triumphant three-quarters of a mile walk from Jordan-Hare after a home win, gather at Toomer's Corner and unleash a barrage of toilet tissue—"roll the town," as they call it, which means decorating oak trees, buildings, street lamps, each other and anything else that might be handy.

"It looks like a snowfall, it's incredible," said one veteran of the TP tradition. "After it's over, the stuff is four or five inches thick on the streets. I've driven over it—it's like driving on air."

Toomer's Drug Store has been sitting quietly at the corner of College and Magnolia since before the turn of the century.

The celebrations sometimes last for hours, fans high-fiving, chattering happily and flinging rolls of toilet paper on a whim. Some break away and resume their tailgating activities, but victory celebrations at Auburn do not die easily. When all is said and done, before cleanup crews can be assembled, the center of town will look like a winter wonderland.

Toomer's Corner is also where you'll find the Tiger Trail of Auburn, a series of bronze sidewalk plaques honoring school sports heroes. Just down College is Samford Hall, an administration building with a clock tower. Jordan-Hare is the crown jewel for a central campus athletic complex that includes the Memorial Coliseum, Plainsman Park and the Aquatics Center. A giant Eagle sculpture stands guard on a pedestal outside the Coliseum and the Auburn Athletic Complex houses Lovelace Museum, which honors Tigers traditions, heroes and special seasons.

There's a display there for Heisman winners Sullivan (1971) and the legendary Jackson (1985) and another for Ralph "Shug" Jordan, the former coaching great and part namesake for the stadium. Jordan, who led the Tigers to a share of the 1957 national championship, compiled a 176-83-6 record over the most successful 25-year stretch in Auburn history.

Tiger Walk is a must-see activity if you really want to experience the passion of Auburn football. But stake out a spot early on game day because Donahue Drive will become a mass of

Quiet turns to bedlam at Toomers Corner when Auburn wins, inspiring ecstatic fans to 'roll the town.'

Jordan-Hare
Stadium
(above) has
evolved into
a college
football
superstructure
with all of
the festive
trimmings.

humanity two hours before kickoff when the Tigers team, dressed in street clothes, makes its emotional trek from Sewell Hall to the stadium.

For the quarter-mile journey that has been made before home games since the early 1960s, the players become conquering heroes, football gladiators about to engage the enemy in battle. Pats on the back, handshakes, shouts of encouragement and tearful exhortations are offered by thousands of well-wishers, many of whom stand on motor homes, balance children on their shoulders and climb trees to get a passing glimpse.

A 1989 Tiger Walk before an Alabama game drew more than 20,000 fans, a turnout that is often matched in enthusiasm if not volume. The parade of cheerleaders and players is slow and engaging—an experience most participants are only too happy to extend. When the parade makes its final turn onto Roosevelt Drive, a pep band strikes up the fight song and provides a musical serenade into the stadium.

First-time visitors who don't think the inspiration of Tiger Walk can be matched will come to doubt that belief about 15 minutes before kickoff. That's when Tiger, an 11-pound Golden Eagle with a 7-foot wingspan, will make her thrilling pregame flight—an inspiration born of local legend.

Tiger's distant ancestor, the story goes, was wounded during a Civil War battle and rescued by a former Auburn student, who nursed the eagle back to health and brought her with him to Auburn when he became a faculty member there. The eagle was on the sideline in 1892 when Auburn met Georgia at Atlanta in the first game of a long football rivalry.

When the Tigers scored their first touchdown that day, the eagle broke free and soared dramatically above the field, inspiring Auburn fans to shout, "War Eagle! War Eagle!" At the end of Auburn's 10-0 win, the old eagle collapsed and died, having given his all in the pursuit of an Auburn victory.

More than 100 years later, the legend lives on through the "War Eagle" battle cry that students and alumni feed to each other and Auburn players in frequent and powerful doses. You can't escape it on a football weekend, no matter where you hide. Some fans yell it for no apparent reason while others use it as a greeting to fellow Tigers.

When Auburn and Alabama meet every year in their grudge match, the "War Eagle" vs. "Roll Tide" verbal battle in the stands is every bit as intense and dramatic as the rivalry on the field.

Jordan-Hare Stadium is not a fun place for opposing teams. The Tigers have won more than 78 percent of their home games since 1939, when 7,500-seat "Auburn Stadium" opened with a 7-7 tie against Florida. The atmosphere was perceived to be so unfriendly that most of Auburn's chief rivals refused to play there.

The Georgia game was played at either Athens or neutral sites before the Bulldogs finally

Donahue Drive becomes a mass of humanity when Auburn players take their pregame Tiger Walk to the stadium.

came to Auburn in 1960. The Tigers played 63 consecutive games against Georgia Tech at either Atlanta or Birmingham before the Yellow Jackets finally played at Auburn in 1970. Tennessee made its first visit to Auburn in 1974 and Alabama's ill-timed first visit there came in 1989, when the Tigers spoiled the Tide's hope for an undefeated season with a 30-20 upset.

What started in 1939 as a field with stands on one side has evolved into a college football superstructure—a fully enclosed bowl with east- and west-side upper decks that hang steeply over the action below. The 85,214 fans who fill the stadium every Saturday are right on top of the action with a state-of-the-art scoreboard providing information and video replays from its south-end zone perch.

Fans who linger outside Jordan-Hare before a game can check out the 12 lighted murals that cover most of the east-side facade—an impressive depiction of Auburn football history. But fans

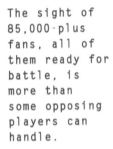

The sight of 85,000-plus fans, all of them ready for battle, is more than some opposing players can handle.

get to their seat early now, anticipating the flight of Tiger, a show Auburn officials unveiled in the 2000 season.

In previous years, Tiger was always visible on game day, whether in her cage near the campus aviary across from the Stadium or watching action from her stationary sideline perch. Fans who flocked to her cage for pictures complained bitterly when care of War Eagle VI was taken over by the Southeastern Raptor Rehabilitation Center and the bird was removed from her aviary

home. But fears that the War Eagle would disappear from Auburn game-day tradition were eliminated with the unveiling of Tiger's pregame aerial show.

Now Tiger is the highlight of every game, performing her inspirational flight between the Auburn Marching Band's pregame show and the team's grand entrance from the south end zone tunnel in a cloud of smoke. By the time the Tigers form their first huddle, emotions are high and the fans are in full voice for their traditional "War Eagle" barrages.

The game is rowdy and fun, especially if the Tigers are winning. A new 2001 marketing emphasis promotes Jordan-Hare as "The Jungle"—and Aubie, the costumed tiger mascot, is ever-present with his sideline shenanigans. So are the cheerleaders and band, which will split into groups that keep fans in various sections properly inspired.

Win or lose, every game ends with an "It's Great To Be an Auburn Tiger" chant, for which fans muster one more burst of verbal energy. When the Tigers pull off a major upset or beat Alabama or Georgia, the players will sometimes return to salute the fans.

On those typical fall Saturdays when Auburn defeats any opponent, it's off to Toomer's Corner for dessert—a celebration that has become deeply entrenched in the football lore of this friendly Southern "village."

Energetic and always inspired, Auburn fans play a big role in their team's football success.

OHIO STATE
UNIVERSITY

BUCKEYES

They come at you in scarlet-and-gray waves, devout Ohioans dedicated to the perpetuation of their college football religion. They preach the gospel of the Buckeye with great pride and fervor, find inspiration through the memories of Paul Brown and Woody Hayes and worship at one of the great sports cathedrals in all the land.

Ohio State football is a sacred rite of fall, a lifestyle-dictating passion for more than 100,000 dedicated fans who make weekend pilgrimages to Columbus from Cincinnati, Cleveland, Dayton, Toledo, Akron and hundreds of smaller Ohio and out-of-state cities. They pay homage to the football gods with food and drink, reestablish allegiance to everything scarlet and gray and offer unflagging spiritual and vocal support to the mighty Buckeyes, who, of course, are expected to win.

And they party. The sprawling Ohio State University campus is filled with festive optimism and expectancy before games and joyous celebration after a Buckeyes victory. On those occasions when the Bucks suffer an unusual home loss, the anger is vocal and the mood around Columbus and points beyond can remain somber for days to come.

Every game is serious business—and the city of Columbus literally shuts down for the occa-

Tailgating, like Buckeye fever, is a game-day staple around cavernous Ohio Stadium.

Ohio State pregames are about seeing and being seen. For party atmospheres, there's no place quite like Columbus on a football Saturday.

sion. Ohio State fans know how to party, and they will tell you it's all in the spirit of fun and entertainment, but there's plenty of evidence to suggest it goes much deeper than that. This is a long-successful football program steeped in time-honored tradition and nurtured by feelings of loyalty, pride and trust.

Expectations are understandably high—and usually fulfilled. A perfect autumn Saturday in central Ohio begins with food, drink, camaraderie and anticipation and ends with a Buckeyes romp over an outmanned opponent, preferably Michigan.

Get there early. With 100,000 ticket holders and thousands more out-of-towners who show up just to share the experience, space around Columbus and the Ohio State campus is at a premium on game day. Columbus, a major city of about 650,000, is nearly paralyzed by Buckeye fever for five or six Saturdays every year.

That's not to say there is nothing going on. Ohio State flags fly from houses and cars, neighbors get together for yard parties, banners urge the team to victory, restaurants and bars do brisk business and everyone's talking football—not just idle chatter, but X's and O's and game plan-level strategy.

The campus, located just north of downtown, is a striking architectural mix of old and new that suggests growth has exceeded vision. The Oval, with most of the old, picturesque and interesting buildings, is the center of a campus busy with pedestrian traffic, and Orton Hall, with its chiming clock tower, is the visual centerpiece of the Oval. You can tell what decades

Orton Hall (left) is the most striking building on the Oval and the Victory Bell (right) has delivered news of Ohio State wins since 1954 from its perch in the south- east tower at Ohio Stadium.

other sections of the campus were built by the changing style of buildings.

Parking lots near the stadium, across the Olentangy River and at various points around the campus are filled with recreational vehicles, luxury buses, vans, cars and makeshift tents that become part of the Saturday tailgating extravaganza. For a noon kickoff, the cooking might begin at 6 or 7 a.m. For a 3:30 televised game, the fun will begin only a few minutes later.

It's all about seeing and being seen. For many years, Ohio State football was the only game in town, and it has never lost that appeal. You don't have a game ticket? That's OK, come on and join the fun anyway. Cookoffs, Dixieland bands, trumpet players, amazing and creative varieties of food, wandering cheerleaders and such local characters as the Neutron Man are typical parts of the scenery.

The Buckeye Hall of Fame Cafe on Olentangy River Road has become a football hot spot, but many of the serious partygoers gravitate to Lane Avenue. That's where the Holiday Inn throws Hineygate, a huge football bash that comes complete with disc jockey, food, beverage and music that attracts thousands of revelers to its parking lot. Hineygate, which requires tickets that are sold out a year in advance, lasts all day and provides a gigantic JumboTron-like TV for fans who can't go to the game.

The Varsity Club, a few blocks down Lane Avenue, is a popular bar and restaurant that attracts several thousand more fans to its parking lot. Activity on North High Street, a favorite bar-hopping strip for students on Friday night, also is brisk.

But if you want to experience the color and excitement of game day Ohio State-style, any part of the campus will do. This is excitement, tradition and color, passed down through generations like a well-thrown football.

I t becomes a giant sea of scarlet on a typical game day. Venerable Ohio Stadium, a cavernous facility on the west periphery of the immense 50,000-student campus and the eastern bank of the Olentangy, has been renovated, restyled and gussied up over the years so that 100,000 fans now can cram into its horseshoe-shaped interior for three hours of football bliss.

By today's standards, there's nothing fancy about the 'Shoe. But that wasn't the case when it opened its doors in 1922 as the first horseshoe-shaped, double-decked stadium in the United States. Design elements from the Roman Colosseum gave the facility a classic feel, the narrow upper deck enhanced its horseshoe look and the open south end provided a window to the world. The south end is virtually closed now, but temptations to connect the ends of the horseshoe have been thwarted. Other controversial concessions to modernization have not.

To get a good sense of the odd mixture of old and new at today's Ohio Stadium, simply look toward the south end zone, where you can't miss a huge 30-by-90-foot state-of-the-art scoreboard that can provide every video gimmick imaginable. But at both points of the horseshoe stand twin monuments to time, a pair of Colosseum-style towers.

In the southeast tower, 150 feet above ground level, rests one of Ohio State's most enduring

The 'Shoe, which sits peacefully on the eastern bank of the Olentangy River, becomes the center of Columbus activity on fall weekends.

traditions. The Victory Bell, which weighs 2,420 pounds, 340 more than Philadelphia's more famous Liberty Bell, has tolled the good news of Buckeye victories since 1954. On a clear October afternoon, this powerful harbinger of good news can be heard for miles.

But the real power of Ohio Stadium is its history (it is listed on the National Register of Historic Places) and the passion inspired by what has happened there. You can't step through its gates without feeling the aura of Brown, who delivered the school's first national championship in 1942 before moving on to coaching fame with the Cleveland Browns, and Hayes, who won 205 games, 13 Big Ten crowns, one outright national title (1968) and two shared titles (1954 and 1957) in his sometimes-stormy, but always lively 28 years as coach.

Woody Hayes, a Buckeyes coaching legend, brought success, color and controversy to Ohio State during his 28-year stay.

Since 1955, the stadium has averaged more than 80,000 fans, most of whom reveled in the Woody era and witnessed the double-Heisman Trophy exploits of Archie Griffin. But this also is the house of Hopalong Cassady, Vic Janowicz, Les Horvath, Chris Spielman, Jim Parker, Eddie George, Orlando Pace and Jim Stillwagon as well as the site of the last college games played by legendary Illinois star Red Grange in 1925 and Michigan great Tom Harmon 15 years later. Remember the 1950 Snow Bowl? The atmosphere, like the football, can be overwhelming.

To outsiders, it's the Ohio State Marching Band. To OSU students and alumni, it's the "Best Damn Band in the Land." By any name, the all-brass ensemble is a huge part of any Buckeyes football weekend.

For a closeup look at one of college football's premier bands, many fans wander over to St. John Arena 90 minutes before kickoff to watch the Skull Session, a popular event that doubles as a band warmup and giant pep rally. Anybody who doesn't get there early runs a risk of getting shut out because the 13,276-seat arena is usually filled.

Sometimes the opposing band will join the festivities for an unofficial Battle of the Bands.

But the primary focus is getting Ohio State fans properly revved up with renditions of Buckeye fight songs as well as the adopted school anthem, "Hang on Sloopy"—a 1960s hit song by a group named The McCoys. "Sloopy" will be heard several more times—much to the crowd's delight—before the day ends.

One of the day's more electrifying moments comes shortly before kickoff when the band performs a silent march through Jesse Owens Plaza and into the north entrance of the stadium. Resplendent in its military-style dress, the band touches off a crowd explosion that grows only louder as it moves into a pregame routine that culminates with the Alma Mater (Carmen Ohio), a flag raising and the national anthem.

After the band has settled to the sideline, another eruption greets the Ohio State team's colorful entrance from its southeast corner dressing room. Led by flag bearers and cheerleaders, the players do a half lap around the field's perimeter before heading for the west-side bench.

On special game days, the band will treat the crowd to a maneuver that has come to symbolize the best of Ohio State tradition. Before some big games (Michigan, Penn State) or maybe at halftime on special occasions (homecoming, the season opener), the band performs its signature Script Ohio formation—a routine in which band members spell out the word "Ohio" in

The weather and the football can be bad, but the band is always excellent.

Script Ohio, the signature formation performed by the Ohio State Marching Band, is a Buckeyes tradition that dates back to 1936.

While technically not connected to the main stands, a south end zone addition has virtually closed off Ohio Stadium's horseshoe.

script—with a special punctuation. The formation, introduced in 1936, is performed to the march music of "Le Regiment" and completed when a pre-selected senior sousaphone player dots the "i" after being led into position by a high-stepping drum major.

The dot is almost always provided by a tuba, a great honor, but the "i" occasionally is supplied by a celebrity. Comedian Bob Hope, who grew up in Cleveland, once accepted the honor, and Hayes was greeted by one of the loudest ovations in Ohio Stadium history when he dotted the "i" in 1983. The routine is an important part of the band's mystique.

That mystique is always on display for first-time visitors, who get one guarantee: The weather and the football can be bad, but the band is always excellent.

Buckeye Grove is located on the southwest end of Ohio Stadium, an ever-growing forest that will eventually honor every football All-American in Ohio State history. Every time a Buckeye is selected, a tree is planted and a plaque is set into the ground at its base.

It is the dream of every Buckeyes player to add a tree to that Grove. And everyone understands and appreciates the importance the fans will play in that goal—the loud, adrenaline-pumping inspiration that can lift performance to a higher level.

It starts with the band's silent march and ends several mind-numbing hours later with the game's final gun, reaching ear-splitting decibels in between. Ohio Stadium has grown from "big"

Intense and loud, Ohio State fans turn every game into a Buckeyes passion play.

to "huge," and the noise level of 100,000 fans in what has become a nearly enclosed facility has increased proportionately.

This is more people than you ever imagined in one place and most of them are standing. They are passionate and very loud. They also can be intimidating for opponents, a prospect the cheerleaders, band and video screen operators do everything in their power to promote.

The "O-H" "I-O" cheer, with sections of the stadium supplying each letter, resonates through the 'Shoe periodically and small groups separate from the band in the second half, wandering through the stands and supplying short musical bursts. There's no need to supply anything when the Buckeyes score, which often happens with happy frequency.

You can't escape a sense that Ohio State fans understand the power of their passion and use it like a weapon that enhances the Buckeyes' chances for victory. And the final score usually pays tribute to their success.

When all goes well, when the Buckeyes have carved another notch into their football tradition, celebration parties will continue well into the night. Why fight the traffic when the exodus will be easier on Sunday morning or afternoon?

It's an exhausting but rewarding routine that will be repeated for every home game throughout an all-too-short football season.

Buckeye Grove is a tree-lined tribute to OSU All-Americans.

Victory celebrations, like everything else about Ohio State football, are executed with obvious gusto.

Every Saturday in Autumn · Penn State Nittany Lions

PENN STATE
UNIVERSITY

NITTANY LIONS

Officially, it is Nittany Valley. By more popular measure, it's Happy Valley because that's how most people feel after setting foot in the "classic college community." Such adjectives as quaint, cozy, charming, beautiful and peaceful work just as well, but State College, Pa., by any nickname or adjective, is an experience that is sure to meander pleasantly through your thoughts and memory.

Opposing football coaches can be excused for feeling less sentimental about this apparently pastoral paradise. Lurking behind State College's Rockwellian exterior is a killer instinct that feeds one of the game's most feared and successful programs. Fans of Penn State University will graciously welcome you, the city will charm and entice you—and the team will tear out your heart, showing not even a trace of remorse.

It's all part of a ritualistic coronation on autumn Saturdays in the precise geographic center of a state where football is king. Penn State plays the game with a blue-collar passion and prides itself as the No. 1 tailgating school in the nation, a reputation that is not lost on fans. They heed the call from Philadelphia and Allentown in the East, Pittsburgh in the west and points throughout the entire mid-Atlantic region to enjoy a see-and-be-seen social extravaganza.

This is Happy Valley. But it's also a wild and crazy football experience, filled with "We Are Penn State" pride, a Nittany Lion ferocity and never-ending tributes to the god-like image of Joe Paterno—JoePa, to those who worship at the blue-and-white altar.

At first glance, State College might seem like the middle of nowhere. Nestled in a valley in the shadow of Mount Nittany, it is an urban oasis surrounded by farming communities, Amish settlements, quiet towns and villages, picturesque mountains and a myriad of lakes, roaring streams and brooks. "Nowhere" is in the eye of the beholder.

The city is an extension of Penn State University, which once existed as a single building that doubled as a classroom and dormitory for students and four faculty members. That building was Old Main, which later was rebuilt into the administrative centerpiece of a campus that now stretches over 4,767 acres with 40,000 students attending classes in more than 300 buildings. Old Main, with a bell tower that chimes the hour, has been the site of protests, pep rallies and many other kinds of gatherings and demonstrations over the years.

As the university has grown, so has State College, which now boasts a downtown area that runs about three

Bigger, louder and more intimidating

Every Saturday in Autumn · **Penn State Nittany Lions**

blocks perpendicular to the south end of campus and 10 or so blocks parallel. The downtown is vibrant and bustling, a blend of youth-oriented businesses that complement the charming tree-filled look of Fraternity Row and the rest of the university.

This is no ordinary campus community. One magazine has consistently rated it among the best places to live in America, another included it on a Top 10 list of "supersafe" communities

aver Stadium can put unprepared opponents in a blue-and-white funk.

and one described it as the least stressful place in the United States. Make no mistake, you can walk down College Avenue and find a string of video arcades, pizza parlors and bars. But you also can go to Curtin Road and experience Penn State's own University Creamery, a delectable ice cream parlor that advertises, "Four days from cow to cone." Football adds color, pageantry and excitement to this interesting mix.

It also adds a tradition and lore that is hard to match. Penn State conjures images of plain blue-and-white uniforms with black shoes and an old-style, no-nonsense attitude, not unlike the man who coaches there. This is Linebacker U., a veritable factory for defensive All-Americans. Penn State's unique nickname combines the first lion mascot in college history with local legend of an Indian princess named Nita-Nee, in whose honor the Great Spirit formed Mount Nittany.

The Nittany Lion became a more visible part of campus life in 1942, when a 13-ton limestone sculpture of a prowling lion was dedicated in a natural setting of trees near

A 13-ton Nittany Lion prowls the Penn State campus and provides photo opportunities for game-day visitors.

the Recreation Building. It has become tradition for fraternities, sororities and dormitories to guard the Lion Shrine before homecoming games, a ritual to which Paterno himself has been known to contribute.

If the Lion doesn't grab you, then the Beaver will. A just-completed renovation at Beaver Stadium, which dominates the east side of campus, has lifted capacity to a whopping 106,500, giving it status as one of the three biggest football facilities in college football. Every seat will be filled on those crisp autumn football Saturdays.

Penn State fans are as accomplished outside the stadium as their football team is inside.

Take a game-day walk around Beaver Stadium, stop at any point and look out in any direction—a sea of tailgaters, as far as the eye can see. Penn State fans are as accomplished outside the stadium as their football team is inside.

That's saying something because the logistics of getting 100,000-plus fans into State College in time for a noon or 3:30 p.m. kickoff is tricky, if not downright scary. The two-lane and construction-filled highways that feed off the interstates and Pennsylvania Turnpike are snarled and congested on game day, which explains why the dedicated tailgaters, driving their blue-and-white decorated recreational vehicles, vans, motor homes and buses, arrive as early as Wednesday and set up shop in local mall and retail store parking lots until stadium lots become

available on Friday.

If you want a hotel room, call a year in advance and say a prayer. Otherwise, you'll have to set-tle for accommodations in such communities as Altoona, Williamsport or Johnstown, maybe 60 miles away. If you arrive on game day, get up early (very early) or risk missing out on some of the best tailgating atmosphere in college football.

Because of stadium renovations and increased capacity, once-plentiful football parking has been lost, forcing some tailgaters to intramural and practice fields. And because everybody is confined to a single parking space, tents are impractical. But umbrellas, flags, creative decora-tions and blaring music set a football mood that is enhanced by anticipatory chatter about game plans, depth charts and personnel choices over burgers and brats as well as full-course meals served with linen and fine china.

No matter where fans go on campus to revisit old haunts or revive fading memories, the air is

Old Main, with its stately bell tower, is the center-piece of a campus that has grown to 4,767 acres and a student population of more than 40,000.

Penn State fans know how to tailgate and their game-day activities are legendary. Food, drink, fun and even a little homestyle music is the name of the game in Happy Valley.

filled with the sweet smell of cooking food and the raucous sounds of imbibing students. The students mesh well with alumni and other visitors who become a big part of their youthful world for five or six Saturdays of every year.

This is a friendly sharing of pleasantries that begins at such Friday night hangouts as Cafe 210 and the Rathskeller, gains momentum at the crack of dawn on Saturday and resumes after the

game, win or lose. Since the Nittany Lions seldom lose at home (they're 194-44 since Beaver Stadium opened in 1960), most Saturday night activity takes the form of a victory celebration.

One familiar face in this huge mass of humanity belongs to Paterno, who seems to be everywhere, surveying the scene with obvious delight. Not the real JoePa, the cardboard cutouts that demonstrate just how deeply this man's persona is imbedded in the State College psyche.

There's no denying Paterno's special status as mentor and builder of the Penn State football program. From the moment he took the coaching reins in 1966 after 16 years on Rip Engle's staff, Paterno embarked on a mission, his so-called "Grand Experiment," to give the Nittany Lions status among the great teams in college football.

The results are as indelible as they are incredible. In 35 years through 2000, Paterno had guided teams to 322 wins, two national championships, five undefeated, untied seasons, one conference title in eight years as a member of the Big Ten and 30 bowl appearances, 20 of them victories. Only Bear Bryant ranked ahead of him in Division I-A coaching wins (323) and only Amos Alonzo Stagg had more coaching seasons (41) at one school. Paterno, equal parts coach, academician, philosopher and teacher, embodies, preaches and promotes "The Penn State Way."

That "Way" has made Happy Valley a good place to be on fall Saturdays since 1960, when Beaver Stadium opened its gates for the first time with a rousing 20-0 Nittany Lions win over Boston University. It was a 46,284-seat facility then, a horseshoe-shaped structure that had been moved in pieces from its former location on the west side of campus.

Seven renovations in the Paterno era have given the stadium an erector-set appearance. The stadium has been enclosed, new sections on the east and west sides have expanded it outward and banana-shaped decks that hang over both end zone areas have expanded it upward. The new and improved Beaver Stadium, named after a former Civil War general and Pennsylvania judge, is bigger, louder and more intimidating to opponents who often leave town in a black, blue and white haze.

Even the pregame buzz around Beaver Stadium can be intimidating, fanned by impromptu

Nittany Lions rooters have been known to reach for the sky.

Life is fun and unpredictable at Penn State games, where wild-and-crazy fans are not always who they appear to be.

pep rallies and Penn State's marching Blue Band, which forms about two hours before kickoff on a practice field a block away, marches to the Bryce Jordan Center and stages a 30-minute concert (Tailgreat) that is heavy on fight song and spirit-revving music. When the band marches across Curtin Road to prepare for the game, tailgaters begin winding down their pregame activities and drifting toward the stadium.

Also fanning flames of passion that grip this central Pennsylvania football factory is one of the most recognizable and popular costumed mascots in the country. The Nittany Lion will mingle among the crowd, well-rehearsed and eager to set a tone for the game after a morning of party hopping at the Nittany Lion Inn and other alumni hangouts.

The first eruption comes quickly, about 20 minutes before kickoff when the Blue Band bursts out of the south end zone tunnel for pregame festivities. Suddenly the drum major runs through the middle of the band to the 50-yard line, performs a full flip and goes into the splits. The crowd goes wild. He jumps up, runs back through the band and repeats his acrobatics near the south goal line.

Every Saturday in Autumn · **Penn State Nittany Lions**

So it begins.

Over the next few minutes the band, dressed in blue with billed military-style caps, will play the fight song, perform its floating P-S-U maneuver, quiet things down with the Alma Mater and national anthem and form a human corridor for the team's dramatic entrance.

By that moment, all eyes are focused on the south end zone tunnel, from which Paterno sometimes emerges early to incite the nearby students. No need, they're already in a frenzy, and soon the rest of the stadium will join in. When the Lion, flag-carrying cheerleaders and players explode from the tunnel like a herd of stampeding cattle, they are greeted by a mighty roar that will keep the stadium rocking well through kickoff.

One of Penn State's most impressive traditions can be compared favorably to a minor earthquake. Off and on throughout the game, cheerleaders will prompt the student sections to bellow the words "We Are," to which the rest of the stadium answers, "Penn State"—20,000 or so students trying to outyell the remaining 80,000 or so fans who answer their powerful call. The stands literally shake.

They also shake every time the Nittany Lions score, which sends the Lion mascot into a one-handed pushup frenzy, and at key moments when the defense needs proper inspiration. These are fans who know how to further the Penn State cause.

The students also know how to have fun, adding to a festive and (usually) winning atmosphere. One of the highlights of any Penn State game is watching the Lion mascot body surf through the student sections, a costumed beast being passed overhead like a rag doll.

It all typically adds up to victory, which is celebrated at game's end by the victory bell—one chime over the stadium loudspeaker for every Penn State point. Then another Blue Band concert gets everybody in the mood for a little more tailgating.

Which, of course, is the Penn State Way.

When the Lion, flag-carrying cheerleaders and players explode from the tunnel like a herd of stampeding cattle, they are greeted by a mighty roar that will keep the stadium rocking well through kickoff.

Joe Paterno is everywhere in Happy Valley, where football is a way of life and everything on fall Saturdays is done 'The Penn State Way.'

Every Saturday in Autumn · Michigan Wolverines

THE UNIVERSITY OF
MICHIGAN

WOLVERINES

It sits with quiet dignity, an oval-shaped fixture on the Ann Arbor landscape. At first glance, Michigan Stadium falls well short of expectations—unremarkable in mystique, undistinguished in appearance and a towering facade or two below cathedral status.

Then you go inside. Through the iron gates, past the championship columns on Champions Plaza, across the concourse, down the tunnel—and it suddenly hits you. The Big House

spreads before your eyes in expansive glory. The aura, the memories, the accomplishments and the passion hang over this sunken treasure like a thick fog.

Buried well below ground level on the southern edge of the University of Michigan campus is the biggest arena in all the land, a grand old lady whose eloquence stretches well beyond the borders of football time. Her patrons have witnessed more drama, her heroes have inspired more prose and her championship traditions have stirred more emotion than most of the fabled arenas in any sport.

On a typical fall Saturday, her majesty will be experienced by 111,000 ranting, raving fans who shoehorn their bodies into her crowded seats to watch the winningest team in college football history. Odds are the Wolverines will reward them with another victory. And, fittingly, that will cap another perfect football weekend in your classic college community.

The Volkswagen Beetle, disguised as a winged helmet, moves slowly down Main Street, followed by a van with mural-like portraits of Michigan players covering both sides. Everything in sight has a maize and blue tint, from specially designed jackets and shirts to the matching sweaters of a woman and her dog. Faces are painted, "Block M" flags are waving and friendships are being forged between strangers pulled together by food, drink and a common cause.

People are everywhere, many elbowing their way through the streets of downtown Ann Arbor and others revisiting old haunts on the University of Michigan's historic campus. The tailgating regulars are cooking, drinking and exchanging football stories in every nook, cranny and parking lot within a mile radius of the stadium. Football fever is in the air.

This is Ann Arbor at its festive peak, and it's hard not to bask in the atmosphere. You get a sense the entire city is out—streets are clogged, people are in their front yards, planes are flying their message banners and it's noisy, kids playing, people throwing footballs and vendors hawking their wares. Local restaurateurs and shopkeepers are doing brisk business, aware their window of opportunity will slam shut with the opening kickoff at Michigan Stadium.

Ann Arbor, a community of 110,000, blends easily with the 37,000-student university—a vibrant and eclectic relationship that eases the pain when hordes of fans from nearby Detroit and other southern Michigan

outposts invade town on a football Saturday. The university is located in the center of Ann Arbor, and the Central Campus area is an almost indistinguishable extension of the city's downtown.

Those who want to combine history with pleasure need only to locate the junction of South University and State Street. It was there, on the steps of the Michigan Union, that John F. Kennedy announced his vision for the Peace Corps while campaigning for the Presidency in 1960. To the east of State Street is The Diag, the center of campus and the original grounds around which the rest of the campus was built. Angell Hall, with its distinctive columns, is on The Diag quad, as is the Museum of Art and other moss-covered buildings that stand as monuments to time. The nearby Law Quad is distinguished by a church-like building that

Michigan's Big House, the largest college football stadium in the country, has entertained more than 35 million fans since its opening in 1927.

Bo Schembechler (right) and protege Lloyd Carr are the latest in a long line of highly successful Michigan head coaches.

houses one of the most extensive law libraries in the world.

But State and South U. also connect the past to the present. Just stroll along either street and take your pick of outdoor cafes, coffee shops, restaurants, book and music stores, clubs and other student hangouts that give Ann Arbor, and football Saturdays, a special flavor. If you want to tour the diagonally shaped, spread-out campus, start early because it takes about 45 minutes for a brisk walk from North Campus to the southern extreme. If you prefer to stay closer to the action, start your day in the downtown and Central Campus areas before heading south—to Bo Country.

The name still is magic, more than a decade after Bo Schembechler's retirement. Fans still talk with reverence and excitement about his coaching genius (194-48-5 record over 21 years), recount stories about his legendary battles against Ohio State and Woody Hayes and reminisce about the 13 teams he coached to outright or shared Big Ten titles and the 17 more he coached to Top 10 finishes.

Bo remains very visible on the Michigan campus and Schembechler Hall, the state-of-the-art training facility and museum named after him, is a game-day attraction on South State Street. So are (Fritz) Crisler Arena, (Bennie) Oosterbaan Fieldhouse and (Fielding) Yost Ice Arena, other buildings named after coaching greats.

The players' big entrance comes moments after the band goes into its Block M formation near the tunnel.

A circular pillar display on Champions Plaza commemorates Michigan's sports championship history.

Like Michigan Stadium only a few blocks away, they stand as glowing monuments to sustained success in the midst of football Saturday chaos. On a typical game day, every inch of Athletic Campus will be claimed by participants in one of the most renowned tailgating parties in any sport. If you can't find something to amuse, entertain or satiate you in the general area of the Big House, you probably shouldn't be there.

Game day activities have been choreographed and scripted by repetition—years of tailgating around a stadium that, incredibly, has pulled in 100,000 or more fans for 160 consecutive games dating back to 1975. Some arrive in their vans, buses and motor homes several days in advance, hoping to snag prime parking spots, and others pile in on Friday evening, looking for any opening not already claimed. Season-ticket holders reserve hotel rooms as much as three years in advance. "If you're not parked and ready to party by daylight on Saturday," says one dedicated regular in the Pioneer High School lot, "you're either a hung-over student or you don't have Michigan football in your blood."

The Block M is everywhere, a sure sign that all's well at the Big House.

By 9 a.m. before a noon or 3:30 p.m. kickoff, Ann Arbor is a smorgasbord of delectable smells and festive voices. Steak and eggs, anyone? How about a lunch menu of steak and lobster? Deep-fried turkeys, ribs, pork loins—anything goes, especially for that ambitious neighbor who's doing

The Diag is the center of campus and the original grounds around which the rest of the university was built.

60 chickens on his mobile grill.

Across Stadium Boulevard from the bronze eagle World War II memorial that guards the southwest entrance to Michigan Stadium, the university golf course has been transformed into tailgate city—RVs, vans and cars crammed together along every available inch of rough. Fairways are filled with flying footballs, sailing Frisbees and every other kind of outdoor game imaginable. Flags fly everywhere, music blares from radios and the distinctive voice of former broadcaster Bob Ufer ("Meechigan") revisits special moments from highlights tapes that listeners can recite from memory. This is a people watcher's paradise.

If it's cold, bring a heater; if it rains, an umbrella or tent cover. Rain or shine, hot or cold, the feast goes on and the pitch becomes more feverish the closer you get to game time. The mass of humanity really shifts toward the Big House about 45 minutes before kickoff when the 225-member Michigan Band marches from the band room to the Victors Lot and on to the stadium. Fans follow the Pied Piper.

"Hail to the Victors!" It's time to rumble.

Michigan is nothing if not recognizable. "The Victors" is one of college football's most celebrated fight songs. The winged helmet is distinctively Michigan, a creation of Crisler, who in 1938 changed an all black helmet to the blue-and-yellow "winged" design so his passers could better spot receivers downfield.

Michigan's "Block M" is everywhere, including the painted one that covers much of the Stadium's east stands.

And no program places more emphasis on rivalries than the Wolverines, who play Minnesota for the Little Brown Jug and Michigan State for the Paul Bunyan Trophy and take on Ohio State in, appropriately, "The Big Game"—the annual regular-season finale that has decided the Big Ten championship between the teams 19 times. Notre Dame (776) ranks second only to Michigan (805) in all-time Division I-A wins and and those teams have played a grudge match on 29 occasions.

It's not surprising that Wolverines fans, spoiled by consistent title contenders and a national champion as recently as 1997, approach each game with a sophistication that belies the in-your-face attitude displayed by fans at other schools. Michigan fans often are criticized for not being as loud, boisterous or intimidating during games as Ohio State fans, a reputation they accept with pride. But make no mistake: Victory is expected. Passion, the kind that has been passed from generation to generation, burns deep and anything short of consistent success will not be tolerated.

"The Team, The Team, The Team" battle cry adopted at the beginning of the Schembechler era remains an important part of Michigan lore today under Schembechler disciple Lloyd Carr—and it applies to both the players and fans. Go to a Michigan game, wiggle your body into your tiny seat and you'll appreciate the "team" atmosphere under which Wolverines fans view every home game. "Michigan's idea of expansion," says one longtime fan, "is to paint the seat numbers on the benches closer together."

There's no telling who might show up for a Michigan football game.

From pregame activities to the game's final gun, Michigan's 225-member band sets a fast pace for one of the most exciting football shows in the country.

There's one way into the stadium and one way out for Michigan players, who get up close and personal with their fans.

Winning eases a lot of pain and any hard feelings about cramped quarters on game day. There are other compensations—Michigan fans appreciate the history of their football shrine, which has entertained 35 million fans since its opening in 1927 while setting numerous attendance records. No posts or obstructions mar sightlines in this massive single-decked structure, few advertisements detract from its powerful ambience and video scoreboards offer state-of-the-art highlights and information from their perches atop the stands in each end zone. And if you've never experienced the thrill of sitting in the midst of 111,000 screaming fans, you're in for a treat.

The festivities really start about 20 minutes before kickoff when the band explodes from the east-side tunnel that connects the field to both teams' dressing rooms at midfield. The crowd stirs to a feverish pitch through the fanfare and pregame routine and really erupts when the drum major runs to midfield, leans back, back, back ... touching his feather to the ground, and then high-steps to the north end zone, where he tosses his baton over the goal post. The traditional "Block M" formation, followed by a rousing rendition of

...if you've never experienced the thrill of sitting in the midst of 111,000 screaming fans, you're in for a treat.

"Hail to the Victors," tells everyone that the moment of truth is at hand.

First sighting is made by fans leaning over the entrance to the tunnel. The players have reached the field and their emotional frenzy spreads quickly through the stands. In the next frantic moments, members of the M Club will dash to midfield with their huge "Go Blue" banner that is suspended about 8 feet off the ground with poles on each side and the players will rush from the tunnel, jumping to touch the banner as the stands shake with the force of a rumbling volcano. A sea of winged helmets pushing together near the Michigan bench is a chilling sight.

The game is a succession of emotional peaks and valleys—sometimes loud and other times eerily quiet. But the students are consistently energetic and fun. They stand through most of the game and take great delight in pelting each other, television cameramen and other unfortunate targets with marshmallows. Since body surfing has been outlawed, they now pass inflated dolls from section to section, somehow keeping attention focused on game activity.

The festive atmosphere is sustained by the band, which breaks into small groups that wander through the stands in the second half, pumping up fans with renditions of "The Victors" and other emotional music. No day at the Big House is complete without the theme from the Rocky and Bullwinkle television show to which happy students and alumni react by putting a thumb in each ear, forming antlers with their hands and dancing happily to each cheery note.

But nothing raises spirits more than touchdowns, field goals and, of course, a Michigan win—the ultimate emotional elixir that transcends cheerleaders, outstanding band performances, grand entrances and all the college football pageantry Wolverines fans can muster. The band's postgame encore will signal the end of business and a return to the tailgate, which will continue in many areas until well after dark.

Typically, it's a victory celebration. But even when it's not, the party must go on. That you can count on during a football weekend in Ann Arbor.

Victory cele-brations, like the famed winged helmet, are familiar sights at Michigan Stadium.

Every Saturday in Autumn · Alabama Crimson Tide

THE UNIVERSITY OF
ALABAMA

CRIMSON TIDE

They call it Bear Country, a legendary land where football brilliance was defined for a quarter century by the man in a houndstooth hat. Tuscaloosa is merely an alias. More than four decades after his arrival there, almost two decades after his death, the University of Alabama still belongs to Paul "Bear" Bryant. Just stroll across campus on a fall Saturday and feel his presence.

Bryant-Denny Stadium stands as a memorial to his coaching genius—on Bryant Drive. A few blocks away, the Paul W. Bryant Museum profiles more than a century of Alabama football and attracts about 40,000 visitors per year. Bryant Hall, a former dormitory, now serves as an academic center and students engage in various activities at Bryant Conference Center. Those with a strong sense of nostalgia can go to the Alabama practice field and see the coaching tower from which Bryant once addressed his troops.

Joe Namath and Kenny Stabler listened to his words of wisdom from below that tower, as did Ozzie Newsome, John Hannah, Lee Roy Jordan and Dwight Stephenson. They contributed, like many other great players, to the incredible Bryant championship aura that still lingers, like a thick fog, over one of the most storied programs in college football.

Bear Country is not for the faint of heart. You quickly sense that special things have happened there and you're overwhelmed by the expectation and hunger for more. Football isn't played in Tuscaloosa, it's celebrated—with a passion few college programs can match.

Denny Chimes, with its bells and lighthouse-like appearance, towers over the Quad and attracts Alabama game-day visitors.

The Alabama Army invades Tuscaloosa before every home game, specially outfitted recreational vehicles and motor homes that start arriving on Tuesday and Wednesday. Unable to get into reserved campus or downtown lots until Thursday or Friday, the owners pay local merchants or enterprising land owners for temporary space wherever they can find it.

These are serious 'Bama

fans who travel in force to Crimson Tide games throughout the Southeastern Conference and beyond. They settle into a comfortable tailgating routine with their air conditioning, full kitchens, satellite dishes and foldout awnings and lawn chairs, and some early arrivals even pull cars to drive around town. By Saturday morning, 600-plus motor homes will fill every inch of available space on a bulging campus that is not blessed with an abundance of parking.

If you want to experience state-of-the-art tailgating, just wander through the motor-home lots at Coleman Coliseum, some of the dorms and designated downtown areas. Television sets will be tuned in to early-starting SEC games, full-course spreads will be laid out on fancy table cloths

and crimson-tinted fans, well fortified with all the comforts of home, will be exhorting each other and anybody who will listen about the merits and defects of Alabama football.

If you want to experience tailgating without the fluff, the university offers an organized party that ranks among the biggest and most popular game-day festivals in the country. Before the end of a typical Saturday morning extravaganza that takes up one entire side of the Quad, 40,000 to 50,000 people will enjoy a carnival-like atmosphere of games, music, food and various interactive displays.

"Kickoff at the Quad" features more than 20 vendors, live bands, a pregame radio remote and occasional displays from out-

The historic President's Mansion provides a scenic backdrop for Alabama football.

side corporate visitors. ESPN Radio has set up live remotes there and some areas cater specifically to children. Fans pass through, eat, listen to the music and pregame shows, observe and try their luck at football-related skills like passing a football and field-goal kicking.

Corporate tents with their own food and activities fill the rest of the Quad, making this a very busy pregame stopping point for fans who walk and ride the trolley onto campus from their downtown hotels or arrive Saturday morning from such cities as Birmingham, Montgomery, Huntsville, Mobile, Gadsden and Anniston, all within a 200-mile radius.

Everything is tinged with an air of anticipation, which sometimes overshadows the festive

Whether tuning in to other games (right) or just enjoying good food and conversation, Alabama fans know how to tailgate.

atmosphere before games against such rivals as Auburn, Florida or Tennessee. This, after all, is Alabama, where winning is a way of life and fans do not lose gracefully.

To fully appreciate the fervor of 'Bama football, you first must experience the deep and far-reaching emotional ties Bryant still has in the South.

Throughout Alabama, you will find bars, restaurants and other businesses that immerse you in memorabilia celebrating his accomplishments. Thousands of homes are filled with shrines to his memory—collections of everything imaginable, ranging from books, signed posters and ticket stubs to photographs and autographed balls. Every time you turn around, the most unlikeliest of fans, with minimal prompting, will recite the radio calls of memorable Alabama victories and regale you with Bear's statistics—323 career wins, 232 at Alabama; six consensus or shared

national championships; 13 SEC titles, and 24 straight bowl appearances.

Every season the Bryant Museum sponsors a special weekend for fans who were named after the Bear. About 200 of the 600 registered Bryant namesakes (most of them teens or younger) typically show up with their loved ones for a tailgate-like party that offers food, entertainment and a special recognition badge. Booster clubs have sprung up all over the country and the Bear's picture even appeared on a 32-cent postage stamp in 1997—one of a four-stamp series that also honored George Halas, Vince Lombardi and Pop Warner as America's greatest football coaches.

Students, especially those who have grown up in the South, are typically well-schooled in Bryant and Crimson Tide football by the time they step foot on an attractive 1,000-acre Alabama campus that has a distinctively Southern personality. But they also learn to appreciate George Hutcheson Denny, who was to college presidents what Bryant was later to football coaches. Denny shares the stadium's name with Bryant and claims the campus' most distinctive landmark for himself.

Denny Chimes is a lighthouse-like structure that towers over the Quad, across from the Ross Administration Building and historic President's Mansion. The brick structure has bells that mark the quarter hour and ring out a medley of tunes every day at 5 p.m. Not surprisingly, even this charming piece of Americana has a football connection. At the base of the tower, etched in concrete, are the handprints and footprints of Crimson Tide team captains dating back to 1948.

The Alabama legacy of Joe Namath, a former captain under coaching great Bear Bryant (below), is etched in concrete at the base of Denny Chimes (above).

No matter where you go on campus, you can't escape football and a sense of the school's colorful history. The President's Mansion is the most significant of four buildings that survived when the Alabama campus was burned during the Civil War, and the Quad, the center of campus life, also becomes the center of every football weekend.

The 19,000-student campus is bordered on the north by the Black Warrior River and to the west by a downtown area that serves a community of about 77,000. On Friday nights before football games, the students will head for the strip on University Boulevard—a series of restaurants, clubs and hangouts that connect the campus to downtown Tuscaloosa.

Establishments like Buffalo Phils and The Houndstooth cater to the students' needs and fill them with the spirit that will carry over to game day. When that spirit mixes at Bryant-Denny Stadium with the thousands of alumni

who flood into town for the game, the atmosphere changes from festive and happy to loud and raucous.

For several hours, the students and alumni become one. It's an inevitable uniting of two worlds in a common cause.

Bryant-Denny Stadium has been a snakepit for opposing teams since its opening in 1929.

Crimson Tide fans do not hide their emotions. "Roll Tide!" The words are filled with enthusiasm and passion. "Roll-l-l-l-l-l-l-l-l Tide!" Be prepared because you will hear this testament to Alabama affections in hotels, stores, restaurants and bars, on street corners, during tailgating festivities and anywhere around campus, at any time of the day or night.

Inside Bryant-Denny Stadium or Birmingham's Legion Field, "Roll Tide" becomes a thunder-

ous chant delivered by 83,000 straining voices—a powerful weapon for the good guys. In games against archrival Auburn, the "Roll Tide" vs. "War Eagle" verbal battle between fans begins well before game time and doesn't let up through the intense and mind-bending hours that follow.

This is war and Alabama fans know how to play that game. It's no great surprise that the

The Million Dollar Band is an important part of any Alabama football experience, from pregame to the final gun.

Crimson Tide was an incredible 72-2 at Tuscaloosa under Bryant and that the Tide (through the 2000 season) had posted a 183-29-3 mark at Bryant-Denny since its opening in 1929. Legion Field, once the site of all Alabama marquee games because of its superior seating capacity, is gradually being phased off the schedule.

That's because Bryant-Denny, from its meager beginning as a 12,000-seat facility, has grown into a college football superstructure that fills its 83,818 seats every Saturday and provides a stately presence near the center of campus. Fully enclosed and close to the action, the stadium now features an east and west upper deck, four spiral walkways that look like giant springs ready to uncoil, 81 skyboxes and a state-of-the-art JumboTron scoreboard that entertains fans from its south end zone perch.

When filled, its stands become a sea of crimson; when properly inspired, its fans become loud and intimidating. This is a huge stadium with a huge reputation for success. And success, by Crimson Tide standards, is always well choreographed.

Starting, of course, with appropriate background music from Alabama's Million Dollar Band and timely contributions from an Elephant, the school's long-time mascot. And that special message from above—a few inspirational words from Bryant himself.

When filled, its stands become a sea of crimson; when properly inspired, its fans become loud and intimidating. This is a huge stadium with a huge reputation for success.

It's hard to hear what he's saying because the noise level is so high. But there's Bear Bryant, alive and well on the video screen, delivering a message to the fans and players who are about

to go into battle. Bryant is part of an emotional game-opening script that is guaranteed to make the stadium rock on its concrete foundation.

It starts with the Million Dollar Band, fresh from a spirited march from the Quad, performing a pregame routine that ends with formation of a human tunnel that stretches from the team's south end zone field entrance to about the 35-yard line. Then all eyes turn to the video board, which begins firing out highlights of championship seasons, great moments and special players, backed by dramatic music and interspersed with memorable quotes and radio calls—"the story of Alabama football."

The frenzy builds and drowns out the words of Bryant, who doesn't seem to mind. Suddenly, Bryant is gone, an elephant head busts right through the screen and the beast lets out two pene-

When band connects with players, fireworks can't be far behind. After all, 'This is Alabama football.'

trating squeals. The stadium rocks as the words, "This is Alabama Football," appears on the screen.

After mentioning Alabama's national championships and 21 SEC titles in an eerie tone befitting the occasion, the public address announcer delivers the coup de grace—"Ladies and gentlemen, here is your Alabama Crimson Tide." The cheerleaders, followed by the players, explode onto the field, through the band corridor, under the goalpost and to the sideline, ready for action.

And most of the time, success follows. From the "Roll-l-l-l-l-l-l-l-l-l Tide" combination of voices and drum roll that celebrates the opening kickoff to the traditional "Rammer Jammer Cheer" that celebrates Alabama victories at the end of the game, the atmosphere is electric and festive. When Auburn, Tennessee or Florida is in town, the intensity is sharper and more sustained.

Anything short of victory is cause for depression, which cuts through the stadium and campus like a sharp knife and settles over the entire state like a wet blanket. But when the Tide has a big fourth-quarter lead or hangs on for a close win, listen for the band to strike up those first notes of "Rammer Jammer," an in-your-face cheer that sends the crowd into another frenzy.

"Hey Auburn, Hey Auburn, we just beat the hell out of you," the crowd chants to the tune of Gary Glitter's "Rock And Roll Part 2." "Rammer Jammer, yellow hammer, give 'em hell Alabama."

This, indeed, is Alabama football.

Anything short
of victory
is unacceptble
for players
who have been
brought
up in the
Bear Bryant
tradition.

Every Saturday in Autumn · Georgia Bulldogs

BULLDOGS

It's a magical meeting of tradition and lore, a place where football is served with unbridled passion and a heaping helping of Southern hospitality. Athens has to be experienced with an open heart and a strong mind. The "Classic City" will win you over with its Georgia charm, then shock you back to reality with its Bulldog fervor.

That's "Bulldawg" for anybody with ties to the University of Georgia. And keep in mind that visitors attend games at Sanford Stadium, but real Georgia fans watch their football "between the hedges." While you're there, keep a sharp eye out for Uga, one of the most celebrated live mascots in all the land, learn the stories behind Silver Britches and the Arch and listen for the sounds of the Redcoat Marching Band and the Chapel bell, which joyously rings out the news of every Bulldogs victory.

To say that football is a fall ritual, just short of religion, in this northeast Georgia community is not an overstatement. Former coach Vince Dooley is afforded god-like status, the names of such former players as Frank Sinkwich, Charley Trippi, Fran Tarkenton, Herschel Walker, Garrison Hearst and Champ Bailey are whispered with head-bowing reverence and fans really do consider the Sanford Stadium field "holy ground."

Get there early because Saturday worship will formally begin on Friday night—a ceremonial lighting of the grills by some of the most serious tailgaters in the Southeastern Conference.

Georgia's famed hedges provide a buffer between opponents and some of college football's most vocal fans.

Uga VI, one of the most beloved mascots in college football, is a fixture at every Georgia home game.

Georgia fans did not invent charm, but they have raised it to an art form. Traditions are honored and passed through generations with heartfelt conviction, hospitality is extended with gracious flair and a postcard-like campus seduces visitors with its strong Southern accent.

If you like picturesque, check out Georgia in the spring. The flowers are in bloom, adding colorful detail to landscaped walkways. Two-hundred-year-old oak trees provide ambience, historic buildings add dimension and the hilly, grassy terrain gives the campus a relaxed, congenial personality. Even the weather cooperates, the yearly mean temperature ranging from 43-79 degrees because Athens is elevated 600 to 800 feet above sea level.

This is a university that was founded more than 200 years ago and the architecture and traditions reflect that. The Arch, which dates back to 1864, is a symbolic portal connecting historic North Campus to downtown Athens at Broad Street. For many years, freshmen were not allowed to pass through the two-windowed passage under threat of punishment from ever-vigilant upperclassmen.

The nearby Academic Building is actually two buildings joined together by an elaborate Corinthian colonnade. One of the buildings, a former ivy-covered library, dates back to 1831; the other, which replaced a Presbyterian church, was built in 1862. Another North Campus staple is the white colonnade-supported Chapel. Behind it is a tall wooden tower with a large rope bell that students, townspeople and alumni have been rushing to ring

> **Traditions are honored and passed through generations with heartfelt conviction, hospitality is extended with gracious flair and a postcard-like campus seduces visitors with its strong Southern accent.**

after Georgia football wins since 1901.

But nothing symbolizes Georgia football more than the English privet hedges that have surrounded the field at Sanford Stadium since its opening in 1929. This is hallowed ground at one of the most beautiful football facilities in the land—so important to Georgia fans that the hedges were removed in 1996 when the stadium became the site for the Atlanta Summer Olympic Games soccer competition. They were tenderly guarded and nourished at a site known only by a select few, a precaution against vandalism or a college prank.

The Arch is a symbolic portal connecting North Campus to downtown Athens.

Even the name of the city that built up around the university suggests an Old South dignity. Athens was named after its Greek counterpart, a great center of learning in ancient times. Today, as the heart of a three-county metropolitan area of 126,000, it successfully blends that

Old South charm with modern technology and industry. Anything Athens might lack in cultural advantages can be found an hour away in Atlanta, but the cities are light years apart in charm and personality.

Athens also blends well with the 31,000-student Georgia campus. That becomes especially important on game day when more than 86,000 fans will bump and grind their way around town before satisfying their football cravings. Sanford Stadium is only a five-block walk from the downtown area and easily accessible from the city hotels and parking facilities not available on the compact campus.

Georgia fans take pride in their predictability. They stay year after year in the same hotels that their grandfather and father used to stay at, park their motor home or recreational vehicle in the same spot, tailgate with the same people at the same time, enjoy the same basic entertainment and carry

on the same football discussions with the same enthusiasm. They carefully choreograph their menus and eating time so they can head for the stadium at what they long ago discovered was the perfect moment.

But Georgia also offers a variation of the classic tailgating routine. Not blessed with an abundance of parking and open space near the stadium, fans tend to gather in smaller tailgating groups at every conceivable location—from small lots and street corners to grassy areas under trees and on hillsides. If you stroll around campus, you'll discover different sounds, odors, activities and levels of passion—everything colored in red and black.

At one, you might find footballs and Frisbees sailing through the air with music and dancing providing a pleasant backdrop. At another, you'll get the recognizable voice of longtime Georgia broadcaster Larry Munson describing some of the great moments in Bulldogs' football history. If you want Munson on the pregame show or another SEC game on a portable satellite dish, just keep walking. "Glory, Glory," the school's fight song, will be forever on your mind, as will the grammatically jarring "How 'Bout Them Dawgs" greeting that has replaced "hello" in the

The Sanford Bridge (above) offers a great view of the stadium as well as the pregame tailgating activity nearby.

Georgia vernacular.

The smells are tantalizing. "Anything that you can cook or eat, somebody has done it," says one veteran fan who typically begins his tailgating at 7 p.m. on Friday. Before his weekend is over, he will have feasted with friends on Friday dinner, Saturday breakfast, lunch and dinner and Sunday breakfast before heading home. Other early arrivals will enjoy the Friday night buffet at Charlie Williams' Pinecrest Lodge or a chili dog and Frosted Orange at the Varsity before surrendering the city to students, who swarm into the Athens hotspots between 10 and 11 p.m.

Saturday festivities begin at the crack of dawn, mixing a carnival-like atmosphere with football fever. You see little girls in Georgia cheerleader outfits, young boys wearing Georgia hats and

Perfect sight-lines, the hedges, a sea of red and black—Sanford Stadium is the place to be on a football Saturday.

fully grown fans of all shapes, sizes and genders proclaiming the power of The Dawg with their flags, painted faces and contagious enthusiasm. Airplanes pulling banners add to the fun and if you really want to experience Georgia passion, listen in on those sometimes-intense discussions between some of the most accomplished second-guessers in college football.

Everything is tinged by an air of great expectation that soon will be fulfilled or shot down on the Sanford Stadium field. Love and war between the hedges.

First-time visitors are well advised to head for the stadium early, stake out a spot on the Sanford Bridge and stay there for a while, taking in all the sights and sounds of a football Saturday. The bridge is another Georgia nuance that's hard to match.

During the week, buses transport students over the span that connects North Campus to South Campus near the west end zone area of the stadium—the only end without an upper deck. Because the stadium is built in a sunken area, the bridge is roughly the same height as the top of the stadium's lower level, allowing people standing on it to see inside.

The view into the packed 86,520-seat arena is breathtaking, especially before a night game when the lighted stadium looks like a giant emerald. If you can't find a ticket, the bridge offers a panoramic view of game action, not unlike the upper balcony at a Broadway musical. Before kickoff, it's the perfect place to watch the campus put on its game face.

You can stand there and listen to a pregame concert by the acclaimed Redcoat Marching Band in the nearby Tate Student Center parking lot or just enjoy the festive atmosphere. About an hour before game time, the band will form and march under the bridge to a northeast stadium entrance, fans following this call to arms. Soon the stadium will be full, and bulging Sanford Stadium is a sight to behold.

"Georgia Stadium, day or night, is a stunning experience," says Munson, who is entering his 36th year as the voice of Georgia football and his 52nd year in the SEC. "You get great vision from the field, from the press box, anywhere you sit. I think Georgia has the best facility by far in the conference."

The sightlines, the perfectly groomed hedges, the sea of red and black, the open west end zone, the middle-of-campus location, the atmosphere—you can get swept away before the teams even come onto the field. And the club level and

Fan passion runs deep at Georgia, where football is played with a Southern flair.

upper deck, which wraps around three-quarters of the stadium, look like part of the original design rather than part of a multi-faceted expansion.

Your visit is not complete without three pregame stops inside the stadium. At one you'll see a brick sculpture depicting figures of football and soccer players surrounding Athena, who holds the Olympic seal—a tribute to Sanford Stadium's role in the Olympic Games. At another, you can have your picture taken with a giant marble Uga.

At the third, near the main gate, you can bow your head and pay respects to the first five Ugas, who are buried in marble vaults with epitaphs ("Not Bad for a Dog," "How 'Bout This Dawg," etc.) inscribed in bronze. Chances are you'll find each grave adorned with freshly cut flowers.

Cheerleaders and mascots add to the festive atmosphere, but you can't escape the intensity of Georgia football.

Uga VI is a pure white English bulldog, a descendant from the long line of Ugas owned by the Frank "Sonny" Seiler family of Savannah, Ga., dating back to 1956. Seiler is an attorney known for winning the murder case featured in the book *Midnight in the Garden of Good and Evil,* and both he and Uga V made appearances in the movie version of the book.

Uga, wearing his spiked collar and monogrammed Georgia jersey, is a regular at every home football game. A special air-conditioned doghouse is available on the sideline if needed, and Uga plays a featured role in every pregame show. A famous picture shows Uga V lunging at an Auburn player, but mostly the nationally known mascot just lies around and sleeps or watches the activity. Uga is so vital to Georgia tradition that he is awarded a varsity letter at the end of each season.

Uga, like the cheerleaders and team he represents, makes a grand entrance. Festivities begin with the pregame show by the Redcoat Band, which closes by forming a human corridor at the southeast corner where the tunnel emerges from the players' locker room. Suddenly the video board goes to work with highlight clips, backed by Munson's distinctive voice, and a Munson monologue about Georgia pride and tradition—the Ballad of Bulldog Nation. The sequence reaches an emotional peak when the band strikes up the fight song and Uga runs out of the tunnel, followed by cheerleaders with the Georgia flag and the players, dressed in their traditional red jerseys and "silver britches"—the pants introduced by coach Wally Butts in 1939 and reintroduced 41 years later when Dooley led the school to its only national championship.

It gets wild in the student section, where anybody who wants to see the field has to stand for the entire game. The Georgia crowd can intimidate, especially against hated rivals when it implores the defense to "hunker down."

After the third quarter of close games or Georgia blowouts, the fans will rise and hold up four fingers as the band plays "Glory, Glory"—a symbolic reference to the fourth quarter, which, traditionally, belongs to the Bulldogs. Their 70-plus percent home winning record suggests the tradition has merit. But when things do go badly, the mourning can last for a week.

Win or lose, the band stages a short postgame concert and the tailgating resumes. Fans equipped with lanterns and portable lights grill well into the night while analyzing, dissecting and second-guessing game plans gone awry or plays worth remembering. It's part of the Georgia tradition, the nuts and bolts of life between the hedges.

Helmet-raising salutes come with the territory at Sanford Stadium.

CLEMSON
UNIVERSITY

TIGERS

You know you're on the highway to football heaven when you spot that first tiger track, a can't-miss orange paw pointing the way to Clemson University. The paws start appearing on the concrete highways about 10 miles out and become more frequent with every passing marker and billboard. Big ones and little ones, singles and groups—soon they're everywhere, warnings that tradition at this picturesque South Carolina campus is anything but subtle.

Nothing about Clemson, a tiny dot of a city in the northwest corner of the state, is subtle. Football is played there with tunnel-vision intensity, football is watched there with an over-the-edge expectancy and everything relating to football, from clothes and skin to sensibilities, is shaded in orange—bright orange.

On the surface, this is a Rockwellian postcard city of 11,000 permanent residents, nestled in the foothills of the Blue Ridge Mountains and living up to its "In Season Every Season" boast. But on any fall Saturday, when boosted by the fervor of 81,000 passionate fans, it transforms into a wild-and-crazy football monster.

Just follow its tracks because they'll lead you to the place Clemson fans call Death Valley—home of the Tiger Rag, Howard's Rock and one of the great mystiques in college football.

Tillman Hall and its old clock tower give the Clemson campus a personality and sense of tradition you don't find at every university.

Memorabilia (below) line the wall of the Esso Club (left), a gas station-turned popular watering hole at Clemson. Mac's Drive In (bottom) has long been a gathering place for players, fans and alumni.

One of the first things you notice about Clemson is its down-home, Southern hospitality. Alumni don't just make the two-hour game-day drive from Atlanta, Charlotte or other points in a Georgia-South Carolina-North Carolina tri-state radius—they savor their football weekends, some arriving as early as Tuesday or Wednesday and others remaining for the better part of two weeks if the Tigers are playing back-to-back home games.

It's not unusual to see RVs, trucks and other utility vehicles arriving all through the week, some pulling boats or jet skis for use on nearby Lake Hartwell, golf carts for use on Clemson's new Walker Course and motorcyles or cars to provide transportation to other points of interest. Early arrivals, all armed with sophisticated tailgating necessities, set up camp along the old Seneca River bed behind the athletic center and then try to blend into the campus life they once enjoyed as students.

History simply oozes from this small (16,400 students) tree-lined university, which opened its doors in 1893 as an all-male military school. Fort Hill is a campus centerpiece, the mansion once occupied by 19th-century American statesman John C. Calhoun and his son-in-law, university founder Thomas Green Clemson. The Hanover House, an 18th-century French Huguenot home, has been historical-

ly preserved on the east side of campus. The old clock tower that rises up from Tillman Hall adds personality and a special sense of tradition, dwarfing the statue of founder Clemson in the plaza below.

But for football flavor, there's no better spot than the Esso Club, a popular edge-of-campus

The north stands of Memorial Stadium rise steeply above the field as the band forms a corridor for the players' run down the hill.

watering hole, or Mac's Drive In, a must-see edge-of-town eatery where you might run into any-body—maybe a current player like Kyle Young, a former player like Dwight Clark or William "The Refrigerator" Perry or even former Clemson coach Danny Ford, who now lives a less stress-ful life as a local farmer.

The Esso is a converted gas station, unpretentious, earthy and filled with football memorabil-ia and atmosphere. Mac's, a small but bustling gathering place for players, fans and alumni, was opened in 1956 by Mac McKeown, who has been gathering pictures of his special guests and dis-playing them, with autographs, for 45 years.

The Esso and Mac's will do a lively business on Friday nights before games, as will virtually every nightspot in downtown Clemson. The tiny city comes to life, especially before the season opener when everyone gets caught up in the downtown First Friday Parade festivities.

One of the most gratifying pregame activities requires only a short walk to the Hendrix Student Center. There, after the mandatory bookstore shopping spree, you can get in line for what Clemson fans consider the best ice cream in America—a homemade delight produced by the school's agriculture department. Rumor has it that ice cream was the deciding factor in Bob Pollock's decision to accept the job as Clemson track coach in 1988.

Clemson Memorial Stadium, constructed in a valley on the west side of the campus in 1942, has not been a fun place for opponents. Lonnie McMillian, the head football coach at Presbyterian College in the 1940s, was moved to call it "Death Valley" when, year after year, his teams were overmatched and sometimes embarrassed by the inspired Tigers.

That nickname, which is sometimes mistakenly attributed to a cemetery located on the south side of the stadium, really took off in the 1950s when embraced by Clemson coaching legend Frank Howard, and it was cemented into Tigers football lore a decade later with the help of an innocuous piece of gray flint. Little did anyone realize in 1966 that Howard's Rock, as it would come to be known, would become the centerpiece for one of the great traditions in college sports.

The rock was a gift from Clemson alum S.C. Jones (class of 1919), who had traveled to California and returned with the souvenir: "From Death Valley, Calif., to Death Valley, S.C." It sat in a corner of Howard's office for more than a year before he finally instructed aide Gene Willimon to "take this rock and throw it over the fence, or out in the ditch. ... do something with it, but get it out of my office."

Willimon, noting that the rock had been transported 3,000 miles by a caring fan, did something even better—he had the rock mounted on a pedestal at the top of the steep east end zone incline, where players had been entering the stadium for their warmups since 1942. The rock was unveiled in September 1966 and the Tigers rebounded that day from an 18-point deficit to defeat Virginia.

A year later, Howard, finally getting into the spirit of his

> Little did anyone realize in 1966 that Howard's Rock, as it would come to be known, would become the centerpiece for one of the great traditions in college sports.

Howard's Rock, displayed on the east end zone hill, is a 'Death Valley' fixture.

The 'most exciting 25 seconds in college football' begins with the touching of Howard's Rock (above) and ends (right) with the players' run down the hill.

gift, addressed his players before they ran down the hill for a game against Wake Forest. "If you're going to give me 110 percent, you can rub that rock," he told them. "If you're not, keep your filthy hands off it." When the local media got wind of that story, a legend was born. And, with the exception of a brief period under coach Hootie Ingram in the early 1970s, Clemson players have been rubbing the rock and running down the hill ever since.

The modern version of that run, assisted by the color and pageantry that surrounds it, is "the most exciting 25 seconds in college football" according to ABC broadcaster Brent Musburger.

Clemson fans know how to tailgate—with every necessity imaginable, from tents and tarps to televisions and satellite dishes that allow them to tune in to football being played in other cities. The game-day atmosphere is electric, a buzz that stimulates the senses that aren't already being tantalized by the aroma of cooking food.

The show really gets under way about an hour and a half before game time when the Clemson band, a 300-plus-piece volunteer unit, forms up near the rock and marches around the stadium before entering on the west side. Many fans follow the cue, and the double-decked north and south stands quickly become a sea of orange.

Anticipation builds slowly for the "Run Down the Hill," which will create a roar that longtime Clemson fans claim literally shakes the stadium. The fans, already glued to their seats, watch and wait as players complete their pregame warmup and finally head back to their west-end locker room for final instructions.

About 10 minutes before the game, the players file outside and board two buses for transportation to the east end zone entrance. Then, as Clemson native Kyle Young, a senior center for the 2001 Tigers describes, all hell breaks loose.

"You can really feel the excitement building as we make the turn on top of the hill," he said. "Then the bus pulls up, you come off, look up and wow—nothing but orange. You can see the fans in the upper deck and they can see you. The place just explodes.

"It's unbelievable how loud it gets. The players are getting more excited, jumping up and down. Then we go through the gate, rub the rock and wait for the cannon. When the cannon sounds, 80,000 fans take it to a different level. I know that sounds unbelievable, but somehow they do. It's almost unexplainable."

The hill is a grassy incline that fronts Clemson's large east end zone scoreboard. During the game, it is Section GG, where general admission viewers can sit and watch in picnic-like comfort. The path through the center of the crowd is marked by a purple carpet with orange block letters

Clemson's volunteer band is an important part of game-day pageantry.

that spell out "C-L-E-M-S-O-N." After the run, the carpet is rolled up and the path quickly disappears, not unlike the ground under an advancing blanket of lava.

"Running the hill can be tricky," says Young, referring to the 100-foot incline that players have to negotiate before running through a human tunnel formed by the band. "You have to be careful, you can't let your excitement get totally out of control. But when you get to the bottom, you're surrounded by the loud and crazy atmosphere that really gets you pumped up."

The sight of a cheerleader rolling the cannon, another carrying a Tiger Paw flag and the Clemson players charging down the hill is a classic Memorial Stadium moment. The band's lively rendition of the Tiger Rag (Clemson's fight song) only heightens the frenzy.

Everybody's ready to rumble. The Tiger has been uncaged.

Memorial Stadium is loud—mind-boggling loud. The north and south stands rise steeply from field level, giving fans in the second deck a feeling of being right on top of the action. A single-decked grandstand in the west end zone and the grassy general admission area in the east end zone provide an open-ended sense of relief from the noise that otherwise engulfs the players.

This is controlled noise, delivered with an intensity and sense of purpose by vocal fans who know how to disrupt an opponent's concentration. The orange is a powerful psychological weapon. Opponents also have to deal with the heat, which can make down-in-the-valley Memorial Stadium feel like an oven during September games.

The place is filled with mystique, much of it derived from the rock-rubbing tradition that gives the players an unexplainable spiritual boost and the noise that sustains them throughout the game.

Tiger paws and the color orange are prominent sights around Clemson, especially on fall Saturdays.

"The rock has strange powers," said former Clemson All-American defensive tackle Michael Dean Perry. "When you rub it and run down the hill, the adrenaline flows. It's the most emotional experience I've ever had."

The noise, said former Georgia running back Herschel Walker, "was the biggest factor (in his team's 1981 loss to the Tigers). I know I didn't concentrate as well because of it."

Adding to the atmosphere are cheerleaders who hang close to the students in the south stands, fire off the cannon to celebrate every score and join with the Tiger mascot for crowd-pleasing antics, including touchdown-punctuating pushups. Throughout the game, the band works the crowd with strategic strains of Tiger Rag.

It's no coincidence that Clemson has won more than 70 percent of its home games since the stadium opened in 1942, and it's understandable that every game ends with fans running out on the field, a tradition outlawed by many schools but still welcome at Clemson. It can get crazy, with young fans begging players for autographs and wristbands and students and alumni simply soaking up the atmosphere.

There's plenty of that to go around, a rock-solid guarantee at Clemson.

Cheerleaders and the Tiger mascot work the crowd, always keeping things festive and emotional during games at Memorial Stadium.

Every Saturday in Autumn · Wisconsin Badgers

THE UNIVERSITY OF
WISCONSIN

BADGERS

The first thing you notice about "Mad City" is its indisputable sanity. It is friendly, charming, engaging and beautiful, a picture-postcard waiting to happen. From the imposing Capitol dome and spectacular sunsets over Lake Mendota to delectable ice cream at the Babcock Hall Dairy Store, Madison and the University of Wisconsin provide cozy snapshots of Upper Midwest lifestyle and values.

That's not to say things can't get a little bit "Mad," especially on fall weekends when Madison's fancy turns to football, Camp Randall Stadium turns red and cooler heads do not prevail—they turn to cheese. The Badgers are living proof that football passion in Wisconsin is not exclusive to the fans of upstate Green Bay and can be as colorful as the changing fall leaves.

Fans flocking into Madison for a Wisconsin game will bring their cheeseheads, red-and-white striped overalls and well-traveled barbecue grills. They will come with their beloved brats and well-practiced singing voices, which are sure to come in handy several times over a raucous weekend. They also arrive with great expectations the Badgers will win, as they have with methodical regularity under coach Barry Alvarez.

Football, Wisconsin-style, is a fun, participatory adventure neatly wrapped in a scenic, colorful package. Whether driving about an hour from Milwaukee or five hours from points in northern Wisconsin, it's a journey that's hard to resist.

Start at Library Mall and walk east on State Street. One minute you're on campus, the next you're browsing a bustling boulevard of shops, bars, music stores, restaurants and specialty vendors in the shadow of the largest state Capitol building in the nation. The dividing line between campus and downtown is hard to distinguish, especially in the New Year's Eve-like crush

Union Terrace, with its close-up view of Lake Mendota, is a gathering spot on football weekends.

of a football weekend.

So is the dividing line between work and pleasure. Downtown Madison and the campus are located on an isthmus separating two major lakes, and the constant sight of sailboats, kayaks, jet skis, swimmers and inviting water offer more distractions than some students can handle. Lake Monona is south of Madison; the horizontal, cobweb-like campus wraps along the shores of Lake Mendota to the north.

If the football gods were to pick the perfect venue for a game,

The Old Red Gym, site of the 1904 Wisconsin Republican Convention, is a campus landmark on Library Mall.

Madison would get serious consideration. Scenic views are not hard to find on this campus. Neither are tree-shaded, columned brick buildings, historical landmarks and traditional hangouts that give it an old, nostalgic feel.

One of the more inviting campus hotspots is Union Terrace, a large patio/picnic area behind Memorial Union that looks out on Lake Mendota. Students go there to study, talk, listen to music, grill or simply enjoy the view, which is especially beautiful at sunset. On Friday nights and Saturday mornings of football weekends, live bands will sometimes spice up an already electric atmosphere.

Library Mall is a group of buildings centered by a large fountain that serves as a popular meeting spot for alumni and students. Everything from political speeches and protests to "end of the world" sermons have been delivered here. Nearby Bascom Hill is an enormous grassy incline that attracts picnickers in front of the school's administration center, and Observatory Hill overlooks Lake Mendota and most of the campus. More adventurous visitors might find their way to Centennial Gardens or Picnic Point, a heavily wooded spit of land that juts into the lake on the northwest edge of campus.

No football weekend would be complete without a visit to the Old Red Gym, a restored former basketball fieldhouse on Library

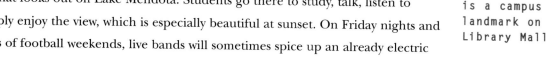

If the football gods were to pick the perfect venue for a game, Madison would get serious consideration. Scenic views are not hard to find on this campus.

Mall that hosted the 1904 Wisconsin Republican Convention, and the Dairy Store, which has been serving up university ice cream for nine decades.

Campus amenities aside, the 40,000-plus students have quick access to 13 beaches, four lakes, 250 parks, a zoo, a botanical garden and a farmers' market that Madison officials say "is to produce as France is to wine." It's no surprise that *Money* magazine voted Madison as the nation's

most livable city in 1996.

Neither is it a surprise that football fits so comfortably into this picturebook setting. These are people who know how to have fun.

Wisconsin fans also know how to tailgate. In fact, they're downright proprietary about it. Some claim to have invented the tailgate while others insist that, at the very least, they were doing it long before it became so popular at other colleges.

That expertise is tested every football Saturday by a Wisconsin campus that is parking-challenged. Camp Randall Stadium is located on the southwestern edge, next to a residential neighborhood, and the few available campus lots are snapped up by big donors. Those who arrive with their motor homes are assigned to Lot 60, a lakeside spot that requires a shuttle to the stadium.

So it has become tradition for people who live in the stadium vicinity to rent out their yards and driveways, which gives game-day festivities a more parochial feel. Schools, churches and businesses will lease their lots, and other prospective tailgaters show amazing ingenuity with their clever use of previously unnoticed space throughout the crowded campus.

Every step is an adventure. Grills are fired up, everyone is cooking and the amazing smells form a delectable backdrop for a carnival-like atmosphere. Fans in cheeseheads and Badger

Nothing triggers a Wisconsin fan's emotions quicker than brats on the grill and the Badgers making their pregame dash onto the field.

beads are throwing Frisbees, music is blaring, pregame radio show hosts are analyzing, portable televisions are showing regional games and everybody is decked out in red. Menus can be creative, but Wisconsin fans generally stick to their traditional brats and beer.

State Street, where many students go for their Friday night fish fries and revelry, offers organized tailgating and many students will gather for pregame parties at Union Terrace and Library Mall. Shuttles carry fans across a campus that is electric and hopping, an excited buzz that sustains itself for hours.

Throw into this mix a special pageantry that has become a vital part of every Badgers game day. Several hours before kickoff, members of the Wisconsin Band's tuba and percussion sections will wander in small groups from tailgate to tailgate, getting fans revved up with short musical bursts. Also making the rounds will be the Bucky Wagon, a restored fire engine (complete with siren) carrying the Bucky Badger mascot and cheerleaders who might do a little tailgating at random sites.

The place to be an hour before kickoff is Union South, which is located a few blocks from the stadium. This is where the Wisconsin Marching Band will stage a pregame concert for several thousand fans before marching to Camp Randall—the official signal that it's time for football.

The Bucky Wagon, with siren blaring, sets the tone for game festivities with its pregame dash out of the tunnel.

Wisconsin's band is much more than game-day background music. It is the magnet that pulls everyone together, the mood-sustaining force that keeps players juiced, fans

interested and everybody happy and involved. Sing, dance, clap, jump and laugh—this 300-plus-member unit will probably make you do all of the above before the day is through.

Watching the band work is like a fine-dining experience. Tailgaters love the wandering tubas and percussions, a pregame appetizer. The Union South concert is like a good salad, a warmup for the full-course meal that will follow at Camp Randall Stadium. Dessert, the band's nationally renowned "Fifth Quarter," is guaranteed to send fans home with a smile.

The meal starts with a band "Run-On" that triggers a big fan eruption, and a traditional pregame show, ending with the national anthem and Alma Mater. After the band has cleared, the Bucky Wagon, with siren blaring, whizzes out of the tunnel followed by the fired-up Wisconsin players.

It is the band's in-game and halftime passion that really gives Wisconsin games a special feel. The band is like a professional puppeteer tugging on the crowd's emotional strings.

Nothing stirs those emotions more than the rhythmic Budweiser song, a jingle written years ago for Budweiser beer commercials and adopted by polka-loving Badger fans. The first chords send everybody into a clapping frenzy and when the song reaches its familiar climax, the music stops and 76,000-plus voices sing, "When you say Wisconsin, you've said it all."

From band members (above) to exuberant fans, Wisconsin's game-day fervor comes dressed in red.

"Varsity," the school's Alma Mater, puts everyone in an arm-locking, body-swaying hypnosis that is broken with arm-waving enthusiasm at the song's conclusion. "On, Wisconsin" is one of the most recognizable fight songs in college football and a crowd-favorite sing-along. But one of the highlights of every game comes after the third quarter when the band launches into rap group House of Pain's former hit song "Jump Around." The 76,000 fans do just that, and the

west-side press box and upper deck literally sway and bounce with the music.

Few people leave their seats at halftime for fear of missing one of band director Michael Leckrone's innovative shows. Any theme is possible, from rock, country and show music to more specific tributes to cable classics, Drew Carey, Elvis and Little Richard. Once Leckrone tried a circus theme complete with animal props, but an elephant stole the show with an untimely act of nature.

No matter how the game is going, you can depend on the second half being lively and entertaining. Band sections break off and wander through the stands, adding to the party-like atmosphere. They might pop up anywhere, sometimes accompanied by Bucky Badger in his

Camp Randall Stadium, which was built in 1917, sits on ground once used as a Civil War training site.

red-and-white striped Wisconsin letter sweater. In the fourth quarter, fans get a spark from the tuba section, which will wander the perimeter of the field.

But everyone knows the best is yet to come. Win or lose, there's always a Fifth Quarter at Wisconsin.

The perfect end to every game is the Fifth Quarter ... what one former student described as 'organized chaos.'

If you ask Big Ten Conference players to rate the toughest places to play, Camp Randall Stadium is sure to show up on a lot of lists. Some of that aura comes from the band and the loud, enthusiastic involvement of fans who can really get into the game. Some can be traced to a stadium that was built in 1917 and, through numerous expansions, has never lost its throwback appeal.

Camp Randall is a historical landmark on grounds once used as a Civil War training site. The old Wisconsin Field House sits at the open end of its horseshoe configuration—the last building to go up on campus before the 1929 stock market crash. Just to the east, standing in stark contrast to these relics, is the state-of-the-art McClain Athletic Facility.

The stadium's west-side stands are topped by a long upper deck and press box that afford a bird's-eye view of the downtown skyline, three lakes and the action below. Renovations are under way for skyboxes and other types of technology, but change does not come easily in a traditional Midwest football factory that has produced such Badger legends as Alan Ameche, Elroy "Crazylegs" Hirsch, Ron Vander Kelen, Billy Marek and, more recently, Heisman Trophy winner Ron Dayne.

Traditions mix well with recent success at Wisconsin. Before every homecoming game, graduating law students throw canes over the goalpost crossbar in a pregame ceremony. Legend has it that anyone who catches his cane will win his first case. The annual Minnesota-Wisconsin rivalry

Bucky Badger (right) is a big part of a game atmosphere that always remains festive, win or lose.

dates back to 1907, with the winner getting possession of the Paul Bunyan Axe.

Those customs form a perfect backdrop for Alvarez, who has coached Wisconsin to three Rose Bowl championships and an undisputed Big Ten title (its first in 37 years) since his arrival in 1990. When the

Badgers are winning, the stadium becomes a joyous victory party. But even when they fall behind, everybody manages to have fun.

The perfect end to every game is the Fifth Quarter, which begins with the band marching onto the field in formation. If the Badgers have won, band members will be wearing their hats backward. Over the next hour or so, the stadium will be gripped by what one former student described as "organized chaos."

It's really a musical ad-lib. The band performs surprising stunts and maneuvers while playing fight

songs, the Bud song, the goofy Chicken Dance and anything else that might get fans roused up. Everybody sings, everybody dances and everyone joins the fun, including cheerleaders and mascots from both teams. Every Fifth Quarter show is different, and occasionally players will come out and join the festivities.

The celebration ends when the band finally forms up and marches across campus to the Humanities Building—and the fans march back to their grills for a few more hours of scenic tailgating.

Anything goes at the band's Fifth Quarter concert, the perfect end to every home game.

Every Saturday in Autumn · Army Black Knights

UNITED STATES MILITARY ACADEMY

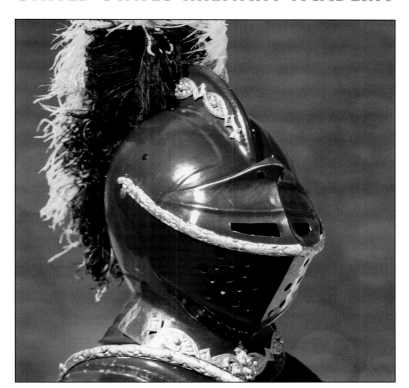

BLACK KNIGHTS

It sits majestically on the high banks of the Hudson River, a stone-and-granite monument to such time-honored principles as strength, honor and discipline. If you can't appreciate the United States Military Academy on a football weekend, you're probably missing the whole point of college sports. It is history and tradition ... pomp and circumstance ... duty, honor and country, all dressed in the bright red, yellow, green and orange colors of a typical fall Saturday.

It doesn't take long to figure out that West Point is a special place. Statues attest to the extraordinary people who lived, studied and trained there. Historic landmarks recall powerful events that are rooted in its red-brown New York soil. Cannons are everywhere, as are memorials and special tributes to heroic men who fought and died in not-forgotten wars.

It's an elegant setting for a football program that also is steeped in tradition. Army teams that once ruled college football no longer compete on a championship level. But today's Cadets are still inspired by the long-ago feats of Doc Blanchard and Glenn Davis, Mr. Inside and Mr. Outside for coach Red Blaik's 1944 and '45 national champions, and fans still flock to venerable Michie Stadium to experience an atmosphere and pageantry that only West Point can supply.

Precision drills, full-dress parades, pregame paratroopers, cannons and Cadets, tailgating with generals—Army still has that No. 1 feel in so many ways.

West Point is all about chills, goosebumps and sentimentality. When you enter one of the Academy's four gates, be prepared for a battle of the senses that is sure to be fought on several emotional levels. Army is power and strength, patriotism and pride, sad memories and hope—presented in a pastoral masterpiece.

The Academy was established by an 1802 Act of Congress, a former Revolutionary War military post carved strategically into the side of a mountain at a bend in the north-south flowing Hudson River. The 16,000 acres of wooded terrain, located near Highland Falls (population 4,000) and about an hour by car from New York City, present something of a visual paradox for a first-time visitor.

The Academy is very gray. Everything is built out of granite and stone, from the stately Cadet Chapel that sits on a hillside overlooking Washington Hall and the parade ground to the statues,

memorials and monuments that give it a museum-like feel. The architecture is no-frills basic and striking.

But it's also very colorful. The changing leaves, the distant mountains, the winding river and all those foot bridges and earthy red paths with no special destination provide the scenic background into which the Academy so snugly fits. History engulfs and warms you like an Army blanket.

Fort Putnam, a Revolutionary War outpost, is camouflaged by trees high above Michie Stadium to the north. George Washington surveys The Plain (parade ground) from horseback atop a monument in front of Washington Hall. Academy graduates Dwight D. Eisenhower and Douglas MacArthur are replicated in statues that guard each end of the Diagonal Walk, a short-cut path across The Plain.

If you want to see old weaponry and pay respects to fallen soldiers, go to Trophy Point over-looking the Hudson. General George Custer is buried in the Academy's military cemetery, and the Battle Monument, the Monument to the American Soldier and Buffalo Soldier Field are other visible memorials. Goosebumps are plentiful every day at 6 p.m. when trumpets sound retreat and the American flag is lowered at Trophy Point.

This is home of the Long Gray Line, a place where time stands still, routine is vitally important and every day pretty much begins and ends the same way, the Army way. But that changes on a football Saturday. When the Black Knights play at home, the Academy springs to life with an out-of-character air of excitement that lasts from first light to taps.

The U.S. Military Academy is carved into the side of a mountain at a bend in the Hudson River (left page). Venerable Michie Stadium (above) sits in the high ground of West Point, guarded by glittering Lusk Reservoir.

The Plain is the center of most Academy activity and Washington Hall is its main building. The massive Hall, which wraps around one end of the grassy parade ground in the shape of a half moon, is a combination barracks, mess hall and academic center. On fall Saturdays, it becomes the perfect backdrop for one of the defining moments of an Army football weekend.

This is home of the Long Gray Line, a place where time stands still, routine is vitally important and every day pretty much begins and ends the same way, the Army way.

The full-dress Cadet parade is a must-see hour of patriotic music, precision drills and well-choreographed marches performed by about 2,000 young men and women (half of the Academy's four regiments) in their striking gray, black and white uniforms with tarbucket headgear. It begins on The Plain precisely three hours before kickoff, and it pays to get there early.

Those fans with tickets will fill the grandstands on one side of the parade ground and those without will ring the rest of the massive lawn, five and six deep, anxiously straining to get a view. Sometimes dignitaries will watch from the reviewing stand, special guests who can range from a U.S. President or Army chief of staff to the president of the opposing university.

You just never know who might show up for an Army game. And you never know for sure how affecting the review might be. The music, the waving flag as the "Star Spangled Banner" is being played with military flair—it's the stuff that chills and goosebumps are made of.

The parade is the centerpiece for a pregame experience that in many ways is typical of most major football schools. The Academy simply provides a dignified framework and keeps everything respectfully festive.

Fans drive in early Saturday morning from throughout New York, Connecticut and New Jersey to tailgate, socialize with friends, revisit old haunts and soak in the game-day atmosphere. Former Cadets will

The cannons of Trophy Point are a tribute to the Academy's long and glorious military history.

From precision marches and formations to colorful sideline tanks, football at West Point is choreographed with a typical Army flair.

be there, enjoying a class reunion or simply reliving old memories, and others come because they discovered long ago that a great football experience can come dressed in black and gray wrappers.

First-time visitors get hooked quickly by the game-day sights, sounds, smells and ambience. Legend has it that you can put on 10 pounds simply by walking past the tailgaters at Buffalo Soldier Field, and you can't help but marvel as you pass those huge spreads with matching table cloths, candelabra and even champagne—elegant cuisine to match elegant surroundings. Ninety minutes before each game, the Army Football Tailgate Show gets fans ready for action on the steps of Holleder Center near Michie Stadium.

Adding to the anticipation as the noon or 1 p.m. kickoff nears is the steady flow of shuttles transporting fans from the parking lots and parade ground to their ultimate destination. Getting to Michie Stadium is literally an uphill battle, but it's worth the effort.

If you listen real hard, you can still hear the echoes of the Army football machine that once rolled over opponents like a well-oiled tank. Michie Stadium used to be a snakepit for wannabe contenders. Now it's one of the grand old ladies of college sports, a throwback football fortress without its onetime abundance of heavy artillery.

Renovations have already begun to

give "Blaik Field" a technological and cosmetic facelift, but if you hurry you still can experience Michie Stadium at her nostalgic best. Cadets, dressed in their traditional gray and black, stand through the entire game and offer loud, relentless encouragement to their Black Knights. Cannon blasts still rock Michie's aging foundations. Live mascot mules, old-fashioned score-boards, official color guards and the refrains of "On Brave Old Army Team" still provide a nostalgic ambience.

Michie Stadium is a relic and it's hard to sit in any of her 39,929 seats without sensing that this once was a venue in which important football strategy and championships were decided. But it's also hard to go there and not enjoy the pageantry and passion of a program that still competes hard.

Opened in 1924, Michie sits high above the winding Hudson—mostly unchanged since her final expansion in 1969. Only the west stands are double-decked and fans who sit in that upper level can look out over the river and Lusk Reservoir, which lies serenely beyond the east bleachers. Stationed on the far bank of that reservoir are two large cannons that will break that serenity with periodic fury.

The Cadet colors of black, gold and gray represent the components of gunpowder—charcoal (black), potassium nitrate (gold) and sulfur (gray)—and that seems only appropriate when multiple game-day cannon blasts welcome the Army team to the field and salute every score. It's not uncommon to see unsuspecting first-time visitors flinch at the sudden barrage.

There's nothing subtle about football at the Academy, where Cadets embrace their teams with loud and rau-cous passion.

Nor is it uncommon to see fans draw inspiration from the enthusiasm of the Corps, which is afforded that rare opportunity to really cut loose. The Cadets cheer loud and long, jump the wall to do pushups after Army scores (one for every point) and delight in tossing plebes in the air like a bouncing beach ball. Attendance at football games is not mandatory, but 3,800 of the Academy's 4,000 Cadets will typically heed the strong encouragement of their Corps commanders.

Fans who have enjoyed the pregame tradition of Cadets parading into Michie Stadium will be disappointed to hear that it has been abandoned, but that won't stop them from getting to their seats early. They will be straining to hear and see Army helicopters deliver the game ball.

Michie is one of football's grand old stadiums, a scenic showcase. For inspiration, Army players touch the Gen. George Marshall plaque (below) as they emerge from the game-day tunnel.

It might be the most colorful opening in college football. Five or more Cadet skydivers, leaping from helicopters hovering 5,000 feet above the stadium, come drifting one by one toward midfield in their black-and-gold parachutes. The last will deliver the ball that game officials soon will hand off for the opening kickoff.

The jump is not without risk. A Cadet once ended up in a tree outside the stadium, and a sudden gust of wind or slight miscalculation could result in an unwanted dip in the cold reservoir. But more times than not, the jumpers hit their mark or at least come close—triggering a huge roar from the crowd.

That roar will be repeated shortly after the parachutes have been cleared away. The team, having received final instructions and sometimes words of encouragement from a visiting dignitary (Gen. Norman Schwarzkopf perhaps), will assemble at the entrance to the southwest tunnel as Cadets form a cordon onto the field. One-by-one, the players emerge, touch a bronze plaque on the wall just outside the entrance and run through the south end zone as band, cannons and cheers collide in a cacophony of sound.

Michie Stadium is a relic and it's hard to sit in any of her 39,929 seats without sensing that this once was a venue in which important football strategy and championships were decided.

"I want an officer for a secret and dangerous mission. I want a West Point football player," reads the inspirational plaque inscription, words uttered by Army Chief of Staff Gen. George C. Marshall during World War II.

That sentiment has nothing to do with wins and losses. It has everything to do with such principles as discipline, hard work and commitment, whether you're playing East Carolina and Cincinnati in Conference USA action or a heated rival like Notre Dame. Academy officials and coaches discuss Army football with words like "character" and "leadership" and insist that the only important thing is "how you play the game"—except, of course, when the opponent is Navy or Air Force.

How the Cadets play the game is pretty much the same as how they watch it—everything is supportive and upbeat from the opening kickoff through the final gun. The Cadets are always worth watching and the Cadet cheerleaders, men and women known as the Rabble Rousers, keep things lively. A costumed Black Knight and mule are entertaining and the halftime show, which can have a military theme or feature the more lively Cadet jazz band, keeps people pinned to their seats.

Every Army game, weather permitting, begins with the arrival of the game ball, courtesy of Cadet sky-divers.

Every game ends with another longtime Army tradition. Win or lose, the players will shake hands with their opponents, face the Corps of Cadets with gold helmets tucked to their side and join in the singing of the Alma Mater. The Cadets will be "standing as one" with hands straight down, a signal of loyalty and commitment.

That commitment will be matched well into the night by tailgaters and other visitors who want to drag out every last moment of a special football weekend.

Football games can get wild and crazy, but West Point Cadets never forget their priorities.

Every Saturday in Autumn · Oklahoma Sooners

THE UNIVERSITY OF
OKLAHOMA

SOONERS

It's an Oklahoma staple, as crucial to the state's personality as livestock, oil and an earthy, no-nonsense Midwestern attitude. Football is not a game in the Sooner State, it's a way of life. From the tip of the panhandle to the dreaded Texas border and beyond, crimson and cream sweetens the thoughts and whets the appetites of some of the most passionate fans in all the land.

It helps, of course, that the University of Oklahoma holds a football monopoly in a state that hungers for any sports success. It also helps that the Sooners' proud legacy includes seven national championships (six outright, one shared) and names like Bud Wilkinson, Barry Switzer, Billy Vessels, Steve Owens, Jack Mildren, Greg Pruitt and Billy Sims.

Few programs can match Oklahoma's storied history, and the mystique bowls you over with wishbone-like efficiency when you visit Norman on a football Saturday. Fans converge from throughout the state and as far south as Dallas to share in the joys of football with a Southwestern drawl and revel in the traditions of "Boomer Sooner."

Stoking the fire of Oklahoma passion is a 2000 season that produced the school's seventh national title and lifted the name of coach Bob Stoops to Wilkinson- and Switzer-like status. It also eased the pain of a four-year bowl drought and the sobering taste of life among football

Memorial Stadium, the largest sports facility in Oklahoma, has a crimson glow on football Saturdays.

174

Every Saturday in Autumn · Oklahoma Sooners

mortals. The power and strut have returned to Oklahoma football, as have the smiles and expectations of those who share emotionally in the rewards.

Norman is a bustling city of 90,000 that grew up in the shadow of Oklahoma City at the center of the state. To its east is rolling, wooded terrain, an extension of the Ozark plateau that cuts through Missouri and Arkansas. To its west are flat, featureless plains dotted with dairy farms and cattle ranches.

Norman, born out of the 1889 Oklahoma Territory land run, was carved out of those plains. When the university was founded in 1890, president David Ross Boyd took a good look at the barren land and began a tree-planting campaign that greatly influenced the personality of the campus that students know today. Many visitors are surprised by the stately oaks and other hardwoods that transform the flat university grounds into a friendly oasis.

One of the campus centerpieces is Memorial Stadium, flanked by the state-of-the-art Barry Switzer Center to the south and the old basketball field house to the north. This is not a typical football arena located on the edge of university grounds; it's right in the middle of a vertical campus, two blocks from the Memorial Union and across the street from the Museum of Natural History, several dorms and the botany-microbiology building.

The Union clock tower, a campus landmark, gets into the football spirit with its musical chimes.

You can't escape the sense that football is important here. Go to the Union clock tower and listen for the chime. It will come in the tune of "Boomer Sooner," "Oklahoma" or the "OU Chant." Near the stadium is the Sooner Schooner Store and a short block away on Jenkins Avenue is Big Hershees House of Ribs, where you'll find a wall covered with autographs of past and present Oklahoma players.

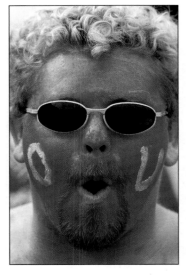

To see the real thing, stop into the Switzer Center, which is named after a coach who led the Sooners to a 157-29-4 record and three national championships in 16 seasons (1973-88). It contains coaches' offices, locker rooms, a strength-and-conditioning facility and the impressive Legends Lobby, which showcases the university's football heritage.

It's not a stretch to say Norman's personality is pretty much dictated by the Sooners' fortunes on the football field. Boyd Street forms the northern boundary of the campus, about a half mile from downtown Norman. But that separation is an illusion—businesses are tied closely to the Sooners. Banners, signs and OU flags make allegiances clear and merchants ride the Friday night and game-day wave that brings 70,000-plus customers into city bars, restaurants and stores.

Customers are motivated by the gospel of Oklahoma football and sustained by the camaraderie of their fellow disciples.

There's always something cooking at Oklahoma, from delicious food to the fan intensity that fuels a championship-caliber football program.

If you really want to catch the game-day flavor, go to the grassy area just north of Memorial Stadium and check out the activity. If you're lucky, you'll catch the Pride of Oklahoma band gathering for its pregame concert or get a closeup look at the Sooner Schooner, the school's official Conestoga wagon mascot powered by two white Shetland ponies.

This also is a gathering place for cheerleaders and members of the highly visible Ruf/Neks spirit group, those sometimes-rowdy superfans who stir up proceedings with ornery enthusiasm. You can get autographs, socialize or sample the O Club's state-renowned burgerdogs and other food under a nearby corporate tent.

The Duck Pond, a city park landmark, offers tail-gaters a calm before the storm they soon will experience at nearby Memorial Stadium.

Tailgating, Oklahoma style, starts early and ends late, fosters an electric atmosphere that carries over to the game and is fun and upbeat—but it comes with a nervous anticipation that suggests more important issues are about to be addressed.

This is not Penn State or Tennessee, where an army of tailgaters will surround the stadium and fill the air with aromatic smoke. Fan focus never seems to drift far from the game at Oklahoma, where limited parking forces tailgaters to spread throughout the campus—from the outskirts of the stadium area all the way to the more expansive parking lots of the Lloyd Noble Center a mile and a half away.

For alumni and longtime game regulars, football Saturday is a chance to stroll back through time, make contact with old friends and talk football, an opportunity Oklahomans never pass up. From Wilkinson to Stoops, the chatter is knowledgeable and enthusiastic and the football ambience is enhanced by radios tuned in to the pregame show. This clearly is the Football Event of the State and it's hard not to feel the passion.

This clearly is the Football Event of the State and it's hard not to feel the passion.

Many alumni will make it a point to stop by the Duck Pond, a city park landmark near the stadium where a Tent Village welcomes fans with food vendors and a disc jockey. Tailgaters also will gather in front of the Union and on the scenic north and south Ovals. One of the more popular game-day hangouts is Campus Corner, a strip of bars, restaurants and shops just north of Boyd Street and south of the downtown area.

One of the season's big football events takes place on the Friday night before the first home game. The Big Red Rally attracts 10,000-plus fans to the stadium for inspirational words and music from the band, coaches, the school president and current Oklahoma players. But for other home games, fans come in on Saturday morning, content to mill around campus, immerse themselves in everything Sooner and soak up the atmosphere.

As game time approaches, Oklahoma officials stoke that atmosphere. Stadium loudspeakers, turned to full volume, fill the air with college fight songs, blanketing wandering fans in the esprit de corps—a peppy prelude to the big show.

Barry Switzer is gone, but his name remains front and center in the form of a sports complex that also details Oklahoma's rich football heritage.

Memorial Stadium is the largest sports facility in Oklahoma and its west upper deck and press box tower above the campus, suspended in a special football universe. In a state not noted for superlatives or excesses, 75,762 crimson-colored fans banding together in a "Boomer Sooner" rage seems totally out of character. But they do it well.

Partly, of course, because of the mystique that hangs over this fabled arena like a dust storm on the Oklahoma plains. Marquee banners proudly remind fans of the seven national championships and 16 Big Eight and Big 12 Conference titles and the All-American Plaza pays tribute to former stars outside the south end zone, in front of the Switzer Center. The now-enclosed stadium, formerly a horseshoe, has all the smells and feel of an arena that opened for battle in 1923.

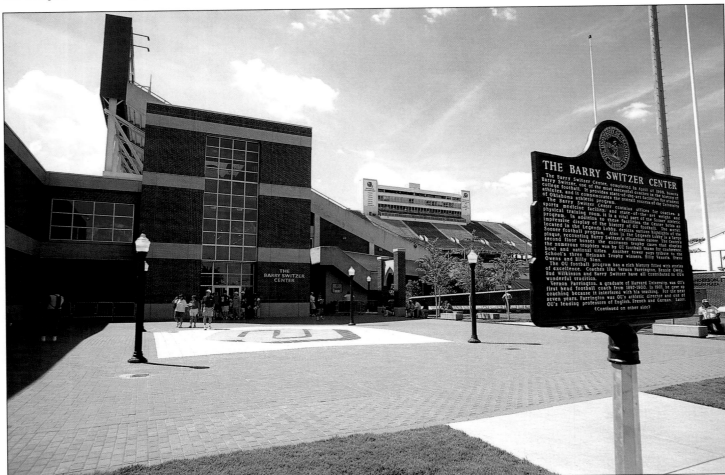

You can sense the tradition and it's driven home by a big-screen video that sets the mood for the team's dramatic dash onto the field. Historical footage of Wilkinson, Vessels, Switzer and memorable plays and dramatic victories allow fans to see that Memorial Stadium really has not changed all that much over the years.

It's still the same field on which Wilkinson's 1953-57 teams posted many of their record 47 consecutive wins, Switzer achieved wishbone perfection, Vessels, Owens and Sims ran to Heisman glory and Oklahoma gained status as one of the most formidable football factories in the nation. A sign bearing one of Wilkinson's many motivational sayings, "Play Like a Champion Today," still offers inspiration from its perch above the Sooners' locker room door under the south end zone stands.

The Oklahoma players and coaches reach up and touch that sign as they leave their locker, bringing a little of that Wilkinson magic with them to the game. By the time they get to the end of the tunnel leading onto the field, the Sooners are properly inspired, adrenaline is flowing and they're straining to rush out and answer the roar of the crowd.

The well-armed Ruf/Neks, tireless and always visible, try hard to work Oklahoma students into a game-long frenzy.

Soon they will, under a giant "Play Like a Champion" banner and seven championship flags—a rousing entrance that sets the tone for the rest of the day. It quickly becomes apparent that the best part of a football Saturday in Norman is the game itself.

Call it wild and woolly, football with a rodeo-like flair. From a mad-dashing covered wagon to the shotgun-toting gang that wanders the sideline, this is atmosphere with an Old West flavor.

Most of the fun is orchestrated by the Ruf/Neks, who come to games dressed in corduroy crimson button-down shirts and white pants that won't stay white for long. This mischievous band of rowdies is ever active, dedicated to the sacred challenge of keeping fans riled up and opposing players bemused and distracted.

Two Ruf/Neks, a male and female, drive the Sooner Schooner, which will be powered on its dashes around the field by appropriately named ponies Boomer and Sooner. The Schooner

Football fervor is already high when the Pride of Oklahoma band lines up for its pregame show.

makes a big "land run" at the beginning of each game and circles the goal post after all Oklahoma scores.

Other Ruf/Neks (maybe 25 for a typical game) do all of their dashing on foot, armed with shotguns that will be fired with attention-grabbing regularity throughout the game and a paddle that they use in a curious pregame ritual. After leading the players onto the field, the Ruf/Neks head for the north end zone where they go into a pants-staining slide, paddle the ground and perform a special chant before retiring to the perimeter. There they try to work the students into a game-long frenzy.

The Ruf/Neks are tireless and visible, but they're not the only attraction. If you listen carefully, you might recognize the familiar Oklahoma drawl of the pregame video narrator. As images of a long, glorious football tradition flash on the board, the voice of actor James Garner, a Norman native, delivers an emotional pitch before finally asking, "Are you ready for another Oklahoma land run?" The background music becomes louder and more upbeat as Garner adds, "Welcome to Memorial Stadium and Owen Field. This is

Oklahoma football."

The fans go wild as the Sooners and their entourage rush onto the field and the electricity remains high for the next several hours. From shotgun blasts and covered wagons to the talented Pride of Oklahoma band, this is one of the most frenetic game atmospheres in college football.

After a riveting halftime show, the band sometimes breaks up into pep bands that roam the stands and rev up fans who never seem to get enough "Boomer Sooner" and "Oklahoma." But it's also the job of the band to get the fans revved down when the game comes to its usually successful conclusion.

After the final gun, the Pride of Oklahoma forms up facing the double-decked west stands and performs a 15-minute postgame concert, starting with the "OU Chant"—Oklahoma's Alma Mater. Fans stay and sway, holding up their right index fingers as they sing.

A gesture that in 2000 was prophetically appropriate.

The sky's the limit for Sooners cheerleaders and fans, who experienced a return to football glory in 2000.

Every Saturday in Autumn · Washington Huskies

THE UNIVERSITY OF
WASHINGTON

H U S K I E S

If you don't believe in miracles, stay away from Husky Stadium. There simply is no other logical way to explain the almost unnatural mix of raw power and spectacular beauty in the most outdoor-friendly sports arena of the Pacific Northwest. The game action is exciting, the views are breathtaking—and there's always a sense the football gods are smiling down from seats in the north upper deck.

And why shouldn't they be? This might not be sports heaven, but it's real close. On a typical fall weekend, the University of Washington is an enchanting kaleidoscope of spectacular sights and sounds—as well as home to one of the most relentless college football machines in the nation.

Don't let this apparent contradiction fool you. U-Dub fans know how to balance business with pleasure and they do so with remarkable dexterity on football Saturdays. One minute they bask with delight in the atmosphere and pageantry of a picture-postcard setting; the next they cheer on their Huskies with foot-stomping, mind-numbing fervor.

"It's always loud," said former Huskies defensive tackle David Richie. "When they start stomping and clapping, you can feel the metal rattle in your helmet."

On a clear day, from Husky Stadium's north deck, you can see Mount Rainier, the impressive Seattle skyline with its Space Needle, the Cascade Mountains to the east across Union Bay and a floating bridge that snakes across beautiful Lake Washington. But what really catches your attention are the boats—more than 400 of all shapes and sizes, some moored to the docks, others anchored free in a huge, watery parking lot.

A spectacular clear-day view from Red Square shows Drumheller Fountain back-dropped by snow-covered Mount Ranier.

Nothing better personifies the distinctive nature of Washington football. Husky Stadium is accessible by water from all over the Seattle area and more than 5,000 fans make their game-day arrival in everything from small cabin cruisers to 65-foot yachts, which offer a trendy alternative to game-day traffic snarls and parking-lot tailgates. This is a major logistical undertaking for university officials, harbor police, the local fire department and even the Coast Guard, all of whom monitor this floating army with a wary, but understanding, eye.

For a typical big game, 215 boats will be rafted to the docks, stacked and organized according to size. These spaces are reserved well in advance, prices ranging from $165 to $500 per season. Another 200 or so boats will anchor free of charge in shallow water and take advantage of the university's $3 per head taxi service in skiffs operated by Coast Guard-rated pilots. Twelve large tour boats, commissioned by Seattle-area restaurants and businesses, will bring in 200-400 passengers apiece with special food, drink and transportation packages.

It's amazing how quickly this boat-parking puzzle falls into place on a Saturday morning. By breakfast for a 12:30 p.m. start, everything will be festive—fans crossing from boat to boat to share food, drink and football stories. By midmorning for a 3:30 kick-off, preparations for full-course meals will be under way with television sets tuned in to East Coast games and radios blaring out pregame information and countless renditions of the "Bow Down to Washington" fight song.

But tailgating is not limited to the water. Washington fans are late arrivals and most will flood onto campus on Saturday morning and gather in the parking lots and other open areas around the stadium, cooking and socializing out of motor homes and under special tents and canopies set up along a grassy area that stretches east from Montlake Boulevard. Smoke rising to the west above the campus suggests a widespread tailgating conspiracy.

The electricity increases with every bus that delivers fans from their Seattle homes and hotels, and an endless stream of walkers edge down the hill from the campus to join the festivities. The Alumni Band, about 50 strong, adds special flavor with its wandering serenades, as does Spirit, the Alaskan malamute Husky mascot that often mingles with fans.

When Spirit is not available, a lifesize bronze stat-

Huskies fans lift tailgating to a new level with their floating army on scenic Lake Washington.

ue of the mascot serves as a popular gathering and picture spot near Bank of America Arena.

Seattle is not your classic college town. It is an exciting, progressive, upscale and eclectic metropolis with a city population of more than 500,000, a metropolitan area of more than 3 million and an international reputation, thanks to the longtime presence of Boeing and such businesses as Microsoft, Starbucks and Nintendo.

Mild climate, mountains, water, professional sports—Seattle, sandwiched between Puget Sound and Lake Washington, is one of the country's great outdoor playgrounds. Entertainment, arts, history—the Emerald City is diverse and enticing. It's amazing that the University of Washington, a campus with 35,000 students, does not get lost in this rather large shuffle.

That's primarily because Huskies football really is a big deal in Seattle. In the not-too-distant past, the school's sale of 67,000-plus season tickets was more than the baseball Mariners, the NFL Seahawks and the NBA SuperSonics combined. This program and campus are steeped in tradition and the small-town game-day atmosphere is a tribute to the passion of devoted fans.

Most will describe their more esoteric memories of mountains outlined against the horizon, boats on the lake, the rain and chill of one Seattle afternoon versus the exquisite sunshine-fed beauty of another, the stroll across campus and down the hill, the excited buzz and pageantry of

Campus visitors are greeted by a George Washington statue (right) at the west entrance and a lifesized bronze Husky (above) guards the west side of the stadium.

game day and the cantilevered umbrellas of Husky Stadium. Others will tell you about memorable moments and games, the 1991 national championship and such legendary names as Don James, Hugh McElhenny, Warren Moon, Steve Emtman and Sonny Sixkiller, a popular former quarterback who was immortalized in a 1971 song.

The U-Dub campus, only a few miles from downtown Seattle, is worth a stroll on football Saturdays. Visitors are greeted at the west entrance by a statue of George Washington, who stands atop a huge granite pedestal, gazing over his domain with apparent satisfaction. Like everything else at this stately university, the statue suggests sweeping vision.

The most spectacular can be found at Red Square, the

red-bricked central plaza where the annual homecoming pep rally is held. On a clear day, you can look from Red Square toward Drumheller Fountain and see snow-peaked Mount Rainier against the distant horizon. Framing this vista on either side are the neo-Gothic towers of the Administration Building and Suzzallo Library.

Alumni also will flock to the Husky Union Building (the HUB), which houses the bookstore, before heading for the southeast edge of campus where the ground slopes dramatically toward Husky Stadium and Lake Washington. There they can look down on the center of Washington's football universe, colored in a purple-and-gold haze.

From overhead, Husky Stadium looks like a giant mouth ready to snap shut on a helpless victim. From field level, opposing teams get a quick sense they're about to be devoured. No matter how you view the cantilevered upper-deck roofs on the north and south sides of the 72,500-seat facility, it's safe to say they give the place a distinctive look.

The roofs reach out over the upper decks on both sides and cover about 6,000 seats in the lower levels as well, protecting fans from the rain that Seattle is so noted for. But the roofs also block out the sun on nice autumn afternoons and create what Washington officials call the "drip line"—that point in the lower stands where fans are no longer shielded from the elements.

The roofs also perform a

Washington fans arrive by both water and land to cheer on their beloved Huskies.

function that was not part of any blueprint. With 70 percent of the stadium's seats located between the end zones, sound bounces off the roofs and increases the noise level dramatically. An Army player once compared the din to the C-130 transports he had worked around. ESPN's sideline crew recorded a decibel reading of 135 during the 1992 Nebraska game.

Washington fans, loud and intense, can throw unprepared opponents into a purple haze.

When fans get to stomping and pounding on aluminum bleachers, Husky Stadium becomes one of the toughest venues in the Pacific-10 Conference. It's no coincidence that the Huskies have won 68 percent of their home games since the stadium opened in 1920 and were 49-11-1 there in the 1990s when they won three outright league titles and tied for another.

When fans get to stomping and pounding on aluminum bleachers, Husky Stadium becomes one of the toughest venues in the Pacific-10 Conference.

Neither is it a coincidence that the horseshoe-shaped stadium has become legendary as one of the best places to combine football with viewing pleasure. Its east end zone, which features a massive scoreboard complete with a state-of-the-art HuskyTron video screen, opens into Union Bay and the 400-boat makeshift marina that gives the stadium its special ambience. The two upper decks that rise steeply over the field give fans a bird's-eye view of game action as well as the wonders of nature.

One of Husky Stadium's more unusual distinctions is a "moat" that circles three-quarters of its inside perimeter between the stands and running track. The moat is an 8-foot-wide by 5-foot-deep drainage ditch that collects runoff water for a football fortress that is only 10 feet above lake level. Small ramps cross the moat, connecting the field to the stands—just in case there's a goalpost that needs to come down.

Close your eyes and listen to the game-day sounds of Husky Stadium—colorful and mood-setting background music by the Husky Marching Band, the "Hello Dawg Fans" introduction of public address voice Lou Gellermann, the head-clearing air-raid siren that introduces the team and the screaming, seat-stomping din that follows every distinctive "Touchdown Washington" call of radio broadcaster Bob Rondeau.

Those sounds, the smells of an old lakeside stadium and the festive atmosphere that hangs overhead like thick Seattle clouds are as much a part of Washington's football tradition as purple jerseys, gold helmets, a live Husky mascot wandering the sideline and, of course, the Wave, which Huskies fans claim as their invention. Washington football is nothing if not predictable.

The band is the centerpiece for every game day. Ninety minutes before kickoff, it gathers for the traditional Band Jam that attracts thousands of fans to a venue near the stadium. The concert is lively

The Husky Marching Band, from pregame Band Jam to the final gun, sets a lively tempo on football Saturdays.

Following the traditional 'Hello Dawg Fans' introduction, the Huskies rush onto the field to the accompaniment of a head-clearing air-raid siren.

and emotional, setting a tone that will carry into the game and the creative halftime shows that have long been the band's trademark.

The music is especially festive on Band Day, an annual gathering that attracts 3,000 to 4,000 high school band members from around the state. The high schoolers join the Husky Band for halftime festivities and a pregame show that typically puts focus on the unfurling of a huge American flag and the forming of a human corridor near the northwest tunnel from which Spirit, the 10th in a line of Alaskan malamute Husky mascots, will emerge, triggering the siren and the on-field dash by cheerleaders and players.

From opening kickoff to final gun, football at Husky Stadium is colorful and lively. Washington fans are famous for their enthusiasm.

"I was there as a freshman and all you could see was 75,000 screaming people dressed in purple," said former Stanford defensive lineman Willie Howard. "Every one of those fans are against you. You face a third-and-one, they're yelling and you hear echoes everywhere. It's a terrible situation and environment."

Not helping the plight of opposing teams is Washington's version of a superfan—Captain Husky, who keeps fans revved up in the enclosed west end zone area (the "Fun Zone") with his colorful antics. Decked out in a full cape with purple aviator cap and armed with numerous props, Captain Husky jumps out of the stands in the third quarter and leads a cheer.

After the quarter, fans look forward to the traditional Legends' Salute—a short ceremony honoring a former Washington coach or athlete. The tribute can be emotional, as it was when former coach Don James, the architect of the Huskies' 1991 national championship, was honored in 1999, and it usually generates a huge fan response.

But no more so than the enthusiasm generated on October 31, 1981, when former cheerleader Rob Weller introduced the idea for what Huskies officials claim was the first "Wave." Washington fans have been repeating this tradition at home games ever since, usually when the score gets out of hand or there is a lull in the action.

At game's end, some fans will return to their tailgating, others to their cars, buses and boats to brave the land and water traffic snarls that also have become Washington tradition. Somehow, those tie-ups don't seem as bad when the Huskies win, which they do with amazing consistency in what many consider the most beautiful college football setting in the land.

Husky Stadium, shadowed by its cantilevered upper-deck roofs, provides one of the most spectacular views in college football.

TEXAS

LONGHORNS

Call them traditionalists. They regale you with stories about wishbones, Bevo, Big Bertha and Smokey the Cannon, serenade you with "Texas Fight" and "The Eyes of Texas," drop names like Darrell Royal, Bobby Layne, Earl Campbell, Tommy Nobis and Ricky Williams and annoy you with the most recognizable sports hand signal in America.

18

If you don't know how to "Hook 'Em Horns" after a University of Texas football game, then you haven't been paying attention. And if you can't appreciate the passion Texans have for football and one of the college game's most enduring programs after a visit to Austin, then you probably need a heart and soul transplant.

"The social event in the state of Texas is football," says longtime Longhorns athletic director DeLoss Dodds. "If you're going to be in the state of Texas, you better like football. And if you want to do business in this state, you better be able to talk football."

But Longhorns-style football also comes with an enticing blend of tradition and avant-garde atmosphere. The campus blends easily into one of the most metropolitan and progressive cities in the country, and the passion on a football weekend is tinged with a creative, cultural and intellectual flair not found at a lot of other college venues.

Austin offers the best in football, but it also provides the cutting edge in intellectual lifestyle. Be forewarned: After the final gun has sounded, after the Longhorns have posted another victory, you might not want to leave this special place.

Austin is the crown jewel of the Southwest, a beautiful hill, lake and tree-filled oasis on the expansive Texas prairie. The 32,000-square mile Texas Hill Country begins on its western rim; a green, graceful aura protects it from the dusty, flat plains that lie to the north, south and east.

Austin is a lively hub for the arts, a culturally blessed mecca for music, theater and galleries as well as a recreational and ecological paradise. The Texas Capitol building, the LBJ Presidential Library, five colleges and universities and a mild, easy-living climate are a few of the city's major attractions.

It's no wonder Austin is one of the fastest-growing cities in the country and a magnet for creative souls. Movie makers love Austin, as do many of the world's premier musicians. The city has its own symphony, ballet company and opera. After four years in Austin, University of Texas graduates are understandably eager to stay.

Because of that infatuation, current and former university students make up a significant portion of the 1.1-million metropolitan area, and about three-quarters of the 80,000-plus fans who fill Memorial Stadium on a football Saturday are locals. Most of the rest zip into town on

Hooking horns with passionate Texas fans can be a heady experience.

one of the interstate highways that connect the state's three major population centers (Dallas-Fort Worth, Houston and San Antonio), all within 200 miles.

Don't look for the tailgating extravaganza you find at other football-crazy universities. There are burnt-orange vans and recreational vehicles that set up shop in the LBJ library parking lot and an orange-and-white school bus that blares the Longhorns' fight song at passers-by across from the stadium. But the Texas campus, with a shortage of parking, is not conducive to the wild-and-crazy parties you might find at Tennessee or LSU.

No problem. Students and visitors can take Friday night delight in the renowned Sixth Street and Warehouse districts, where numerous restaurants feed the body and many of the city's more than 100 music clubs feed the soul. You can get everything from blues, jazz and country to rock and rap in this festival of music—Bourbon Street without the strip clubs.

Saturday arrivals will flock to such campus hangouts as the Posse East, just north of the stadium, and Scholz Bier Garten, a hot spot that offers barbecue and beer to the south of the facility. For those who don't want to stray too far from the stadium, the Texas Club and other party suites help everybody get properly revved up for football.

The renovated Memorial Stadium horseshoe has played a big part in Texas' football revival.

Texas fans love their traditions, which include a longhorn named Bevo (above) and a cannon appropriately called Smokey.

exans love their traditions. They love the symbolism, the stories behind them and the way they connect generations and promote teamwork. Tradition is at the very core of Longhorns football and it's the lifeblood of a winning legacy.

The Texas legacy began innocently enough in 1894 when R.D. Wentworth was paid $325 and coached the first Longhorns team to a 6-1 record. It was raised to a higher level 22 coaches later when Royal, a 32-year-old former Oklahoma star, took the job and began a 20-year reign (1957-76) that produced a 167-47-5 record, 11 Southwest Conference titles and three full or shared national championships.

It was Royal who introduced the wishbone offense to college football in 1968 and it was Royal who lifted Texas football to status among the great programs in the college game. His 1969 team was proclaimed national champion by no less an authority than U.S. President Richard M. Nixon. Royal's sayings—"You dance with who brung ya"—are locked securely into Longhorns lore and he remains today as a visible Texas ambassador and link to the past.

Like Royal, many of the Texas traditions are visible reminders:

■ The 27-story Main Building is the centerpiece of the largest single-site campus in the country (more than 50,000 students). The so-called Texas Tower was a symbol of infamy in 1966 when Charles Whitman climbed to the top and shot 44 persons on the campus below, killing 13. But the one-time library now houses administrative offices and serves as a beacon to Longhorns athletic success. After a football victory or a Big 12 team championship is won, the tower will be bathed in orange lights. When Texas claims a national title, as it did in 1963, 1969 and 1970, a large numeral "1" will light up on each side.

■ The Texas Longhorn has been the school's official mascot since the early 1900s, but Bevo has been a fixture at Texas games only since 1966. Look into the end zone during a game and you'll see Bevo, a genuine Longhorn, attended by the Silver Spurs service organization.

■ Look for Big Bertha, the largest, loudest bass drum in the world, whenever the University of Texas band performs. You can't miss her because Bertha weighs 500 pounds, measures 54 inches in diameter and needs a wheeled

trailer and eight energetic attendants to maneuver her around the field. Big Bertha was introduced to Texas students in 1955.

■ Brace yourself or Smokey will knock you right out of your seat. The cannon, attended by the Texas Cowboys organization, fires two blank 10-gauge shotgun shells at the beginning, the half and the end of every game and after every Longhorns score.

■ Texas fans have been flashing their "Hook 'Em Horns" sign since 1955, thanks to a creative former head cheerleader named Harley Clark.

■ The Hex Rally, an annual candle-lighting ritual that dates back to 1941, precedes every game against the hated Aggies of Texas A&M. The touching Friday night event begins when a cheerleader lights a single candle from a flame on an outdoor stage near the Tower and passes it around the crowd as a single trumpet player begins playing "The Eyes of Texas." Every time through the song, more band members join until everyone is either playing or singing. Another annual rally is the Torchlight Parade, which draws thousands to the campus before every Oklahoma game.

When you see the Texas Tower bathed in orange with a lighted '1' on each side, you know the Longhorns have won a national championship.

The traditional Torchlight Parade draws thousands of fans to campus before the Oklahoma game.

"Come early, be loud, stay late." If you don't, you probably will miss something big in Mack Brown's remarkable Texas football revival. Since Brown took the coaching reins in 1998 and began issuing his motivational challenges ("Wear Orange with pride"), the Longhorns have posted a 16-2 home record and rekindled memories of the Royal and Fred Akers eras.

If you don't know how to 'Hook 'Em Horns' after a University of Texas football game, then you haven't been paying attention.

The fans love Brown's attention to public relations detail and tradition. They also like a recently completed Memorial Stadium renovation that has aided Brown's cause. The field was lowered by 6 feet, the track once used for the nationally renowned Texas Relays was removed and the intimidation factor was increased dramatically.

The oddly configured, horseshoe-shaped facility, with 80,000-plus fans rocking and rolling in a sea of burnt orange and white, is loud and demoralizing, as the No. 3-ranked Nebraska Cornhuskers discovered in a 1999 upset loss to the Longhorns. With the stadium double-decked on both sides and singled-decked in the north end zone, the fans now are closer to the field and a consistently disruptive influence for opposing offenses. The state-of-the-art JumboTron scoreboard, located above the Moncrief-Neuhaus Athletics Center at the open end of the horseshoe, stands as both an example of modern technology and a tribute to the past.

The stadium scoreboard was dedicated in 1972 to the memory of Freddie Steinmark, a starting safety on Texas' 1969 national championship team who became a national symbol of courage and determination. Steinmark played in the Longhorns' memorable 15-14 championship-clinching win over Arkansas six days before receiving a diagnosis of bone cancer that eventually forced amputation of his left leg. He remained a visible presence on campus until his death in 1971.

Thirty years later, Steinmark is part of a recurring Texas ritual. Before every game, players walk from their locker room down a hallway that contains pictures of every Longhorns All-American, pausing to touch a set of mounted Longhorns while thinking about those players and their great pride. When they pass the scoreboard on their way to the field, they pause again to touch a picture of Steinmark, hoping that his courage can inspire them to great performances.

It often does.

No Texas game would be complete without the attention-getting rumbles of Big Bertha, a 500-pound bass drum that is pulled around on a special trailer.

Burnt orange is the color of choice at Texas games and fan passion is stoked by the team's wild, smoke-screened dash (below) into Memorial Stadium before the opening kickoff.

The electricity really picks up about two hours before game time when a bus delivers the Texas team to the north entrance of the stadium, where players are greeted by thousands of excited fans. The players walk into the stadium, cross the middle of the field from end zone to end zone and enter their locker room. Soon the nearly empty stadium will be jumping.

And that means the Texas band, known throughout the state and points beyond as the Show  Band of the Southwest, will be performing its magic. Outfitted in western-cut uniforms and cowboy hats, band members take the lead on one of the most dramatic opening acts in college football.

Minutes before kickoff, the band enters the stadium through the north tunnel and goes into its brief pregame show. The real fun begins when it forms the traditional block-T formation, trunk facing the south-end canopy where the players will enter the field into a human corridor.

The first roar of the crowd greets APO service fraternity members when they run onto the field with a giant Texas flag that covers almost half the field. Then every Texas fan, his hand forming a "Hook 'Em Horns" sign, raises his arm skyward and sings "The Eyes of Texas." This tear-jerking moment fades quickly when the JumboTron goes into action.

Suddenly there's a herd of animated Longhorns running through the streets of Austin, across campus and into the tunnel as the crowd builds to the moment. Just when it appears the animated Longhorns are going to explode onto the field, the band goes into the Texas fight song and the real Longhorns burst forth from the canopy amid a cloud of smoke. By the time the team reaches its west-side bench, both fans and players are in a frenzy.

And so it goes. The "Texas" ... "Fight" cheer, with one side of the stadium responding to the other, will fill the air periodically and students will stand, cheer and body surf from opening kick-off to the end. The band vigorously works the crowd, delivers timely renditions of "Yellow Rose of Texas" and "Wabash Cannonball" and performs a halftime show that keeps fans glued to their seats. Success breeds passion, and you can usually anticipate plenty of both at Memorial Stadium.

A Mack Brown-inspired tradition brings the day's festivities to a fitting close when he leads his players to the band near the student section, extends his horn-hooking hand skyward and joins for a final rendition of "The Eyes of Texas."

The message comes through loud and clear.

The moment of truth for every Texas player is that tunnel pause that precedes an emotional dash onto the field.

Every Saturday in Autumn · Florida State Seminoles

FLORIDA STATE
UNIVERSITY

SEMINOLES

The excitement builds like a giant wave. First comes the anticipatory buzz as captains gather for the pregame coin toss, then a chilling hum that grows louder with the first methodical strains of the war chant. During the short pause that follows the midfield conference, tension is so thick that Doak Campbell Stadium is ready to boil.

Suddenly, Chief Osceola bolts from the south end zone, a lone horseman on an Appaloosa holding a flaming spear high in his right hand. The crowd erupts as he charges straight to midfield, rears the horse on its heels and spikes the spear in the middle of the giant Seminole-head logo. Symbolically, Chief Osceola is delivering a dagger to the heart of every opposing player.

Such is the state of Florida State University football that daggers are delivered in many ways on football Saturday nights in Tallahassee. But none more dramatically than Chief Osceola's ride aboard Renegade in one of college football's most spectacular game openings.

This is a program that can kill you softly with its championship aura, symbolically with its flaming spear or literally with its superior athleticism. But it also can warm you with its Southern charm and enchant you with its heart-tugging traditions.

Chief Osceola and Renegade fire up fans with a pregame spike.

Football weekend in Tallahassee is a many-splendored thing, from a spirited downtown rally on Friday night to the players' prayer that follows every game. And if it comes across as a giant victory celebration, there's good reason: The Seminoles have not lost at Doak Campbell Stadium since 1991, an unbeaten streak that reached 52 in the 2000 season.

Tallahassee is a mind-numbing experience. Its rolling hills, canopy roads, moss-draped oaks, flowering azaleas, snowy dogwoods, towering pines and shimmering lakes and springs will charm and overwhelm you; its sometimes incongruous combination of politics, rattlesnake roundups, history and sprawling plantations will surprise and amaze you.

There's no mistaking the Southern feel of this 140,000-population city located only 14 miles from the Georgia border at the foothills of the Appalachian

Mountains. Likewise, it's hard not to feel the Gulf Coast breezes and more tropical climate that link Tallahassee physically to its neighbors on the Florida panhandle and peninsula. This is a city torn between two worlds.

But it's also a city with clearly defined passions. As the government center of the state, this is a place where life-bettering laws and momentous decisions are made. As the heart of Seminole country, this is home of one of the most extraordinary football machines in all the land. The football passion is just as visible as the state Capitol dome that towers above the Tallahassee landscape.

Buildings throughout the area sport images of Chief Osceola and area bars, restaurants and other businesses tie themselves both in name (Seminole this, Seminole that) and spirit to the Florida State football experience. Apparel stores do a booming business here, as do tattoo and T-shirt shops. Just try to listen to the

radio, wander through a grocery store or get through a typical workday without hearing excerpts from the gospel of coach Bobby Bowden—at any time of the year.

Every Friday night before home games, a three-block stretch of Adams Street in the shadow of the Capitol building is closed off to traffic for the "Downtown Get-Down"—a pep rally-like celebration to which students, alumni, cheerleaders and band members flock for live music, refreshment and football-related entertainment. For several hours, the center of Florida government provides a stately backdrop for Seminoles fever—a role it also will play the next day.

Football really is that important here. Fans literally schedule their life around it and on typical fall Saturdays, the entire city transforms into "Noleville." From as far away as Atlanta and Miami, they come to the Magic Kingdom of North Florida—a place where national championship dreams come true and football fantasies are nourished and fulfilled.

And the good guys always win.

Two Florida State fixtures: the scenic Westcott fountain (top photo) and football coach/folk hero Bobby Bowden.

FSU passion can be measured in different ways, from the more visible fan fervor (below) to the Sod Cemetery tradition (above) that began in 1962 with a win at Georgia.

Jeb Bush officially presides over the state of Florida from Tallahassee's Governor's Mansion, but the city really belongs to Bowden. That's Coach Bowden to a legion of admirers, who hang his picture on walls for inspiration, reverently quote his down-home words and Christian philosophies, praise his sleek, wide-open coaching style and embrace his ever-growing status as a Southern folk hero.

Success breeds admiration and Bowden has earned plenty of that. The Seminoles have won more than 80 percent of their games and claimed two national championships in his quarter century at Tallahassee. In the 14 seasons from 1987 through 2000, the Seminoles never failed to win at least 10 games and they have won every Atlantic Coast Conference title since becoming an eligible league member in 1992. Florida State won 109 games in the 1990s, more than any team in a single decade—ever.

"I just love to coach," Bowden says, and that "love" has helped transform Florida State into one of the most passionate programs in the country. A former women's college that didn't even play its first football game until 1947, Florida State can match success, traditions and support with teams that have been playing since the turn of the century. FSU fans call their passion Saturday Night Fever.

Because of the energy-sapping September and October heat, most games are played on Saturday nights and the serious outdoor tailgaters, many armed with generators and air-circulating fans, don't get started until four hours before kickoff. But what FSU tailgates might lack in longevity they more than make up for with enthusiasm.

Everything builds suddenly, almost like magic, as the buzz and electricity that have filled the air all day escalate into a festive celebration. The three-block stretch of College Avenue that connects the 35,000-student campus to the Capitol becomes a crowded walkway. Fans pack parking lots and set up grills, line up to visit FSU's Sod Cemetery, venture out from the air-conditioned comfort of Bullwinkles Tavern and other area bars and restaurants, picnic on Landis Green,

visit old campus haunts and update their Seminoles wardrobe at Bill's Bookstore and the Garnet & Gold shop.

The Langford Green, a large grassy area, becomes the real center for pregame activity just south of Doak Campbell Stadium. This is where cheerleaders assemble and the Marching Chiefs regroup after entertaining 5,000 fans in a pregame concert at Dick Howser Stadium. Interactive displays attract kids and corporate tents feed and entertain curious wanderers.

Everywhere you go, "Spirit Hunters" will offer to paint your face and shouts of "F-S-U" will fill the air. The war chant, Florida State's signature battle cry, also makes its first appearance during tailgating as a hum-like, monotone backdrop for the day's events. Get used to it. The more friendly sounds of pregame shows, fight-song music, televised games and your basic, everyday football chatter is served up with heaping helpings of chicken, ribs, burgers and potato salad.

The university's Gothic architecture, sprawling oaks and flowery, nostalgic feel give this tail-gate a Southern accent and the 455-acre campus, from its arched Westcott gate and fountain on the east side to the University Center complex at Doak Campbell on the southwest, is blanketed

The University Center complex wraps around the exterior of Doak Campbell Stadium, hiding its fall Saturday football identity.

by a sense of anticipation—and invincibility.

Florida State fans get to their seats early to watch the band serenade players during a helmet-raising 'ankle walk' warmup routine.

From the outside, Doak Campbell Stadium is hard to spot. It's cloaked on three sides by the massive University Center that wraps around its exterior and on the fourth by the Moore Athletics Center, which houses its football offices, locker room and strength and conditioning area. Once chided for its erector-set look, the stadium has evolved into a state-of-the-art facility.

The huge University Center, a complex that houses offices and student services, is physically connected to Doak Campbell, the back of the Center forming the outside of the stadium. The red-brick Gothic look blends subtly into the rest of campus and the enclosed single-decked stadium now features skyboxes, a "War Board" video system perched above the north end zone and 80,000 seats that are filled every Saturday, making life uncomfortable for already-overheated opponents.

Outside the complex on a west-side plaza is the Sportsmanship sculpture, a double-lifesize football player reaching down to help up a defeated opponent. To the north of the stadium,

The war chant, FSU's signature battle cry, is usually accompanied by an up-and-down hand motion.

next to the practice fields across from the Moore Center, is the Sod Cemetery—a special Florida State tradition that dates back to 1962 when the Seminoles surprised Georgia, 18-0, at Sanford Stadium.

At one time, it was customary for Florida State captains to bring back a chunk of sod from the opposing stadium when the Seminoles recorded an upset win on the road. In recent years, since FSU is usually the favorite wherever it plays, "sod games" have been designated by Bowden, who coordinates the turf-gathering efforts himself. This has become serious business.

When the Seminoles record a designated win or a bowl victory, bronze tombstones with concrete casing are ordered from West Virginia and the sod is buried under an inscription that gives the score and date. Before every home game, the cemetery (70 graves through 2000) is cleaned up and flowers are placed on tombstones matching that day's opponent—color coordinated, of course.

The Chief Osceola-Renegade pregame show also is serious business. Renegade's stadium arrival, with a large entourage of handlers, is signaled by the siren of a Leon County Sheriff Department escort about two hours before kickoff. Early-arriving fans will gather under the north stands just to watch the Chief and Renegade get dressed up for the ceremony.

Everybody else will be seated when the warmups begin. The first of many crowd roars will

Before Chief Osceola's flaming spear is doused at midfield, Florida State fans will have been treated to a myriad of sights and sounds that give Seminoles football a distinctive flavor.

Florida State players and fans are well versed on postgame celebrations, from the subtle variety (below) to the more hearty displays of emotion (opposite page).

come when the Seminole players line up across the field at the 50-yard line, lift their gold helmets above their heads and begin walking gingerly on the sides of their feet (a stretching exercise) toward the end zone as the Marching Chiefs play the theme from "The Good, the Bad and the Ugly." When the players reach the end zone, they turn and run to Bowden at the 20 as the band switches to the FSU fight song.

The "Ankle Walk" is only an appetizer. Before Chief Osceola's flaming spear is doused at midfield, Florida State fans will have been treated to a myriad of sights and sounds that give Seminoles football its distinctive flavor.

The first barrage comes about a half hour before kickoff when the War Board presents a choreographed show featuring animated helmet battles, great plays and memorable moments with emotion-tugging background music. Then the Marching Chiefs do their part with a lively pregame show that camouflages the arrival of Chief Osceola and Renegade in the north end zone.

By this point, anticipation is high. War Board images of revved-up players making their way through the tunnel, cheerleaders standing at the field entrance with a run-through Seminole-head banner and the Chief with his flaming spear only heighten the tension.

Suddenly, Bowden gives the signal and tension explodes in garnet-and-gold fury. The players burst through the banner and a corridor of band members as Chief Osceola rides frantically to the south end zone, where he turns and faces midfield. Soon the roar fades and the team captains move to the 50-yard line, setting the stage for the Chief's grand spear-throwing finale.

From the moment the players burst onto the field through the postgame prayer, Florida State

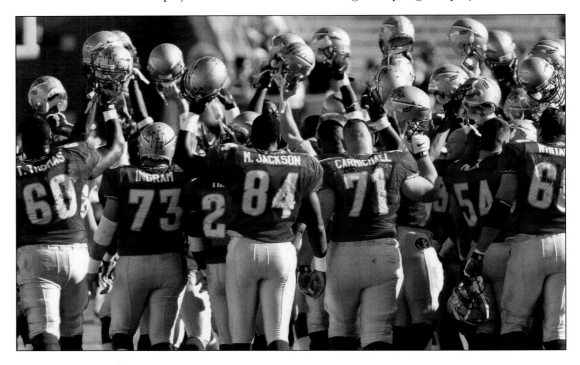

football is a loud, mind-numbing succession of war chants, "F-S-U" cheers, touchdown celebrations and fiery band music. Students stand for the entire game in the northwest end zone area—few of which have ever witnessed a Seminoles loss.

Sometimes the war chant, accompanied by a chopping arm motion, will be started by the band. Other times the students will get it going and sometimes, if a big play or defensive stand is needed, the players on the sideline will do the honors.

Doak Campbell Stadium runs on emotion and the band and players supply ample doses to keep everything hopping. After the Marching Chiefs finish their halftime show, they break into wandering pep squads. At the end of the third quarter, they play "The Good, the Bad and the Ugly" again as players and fans hold up four fingers—a symbolic statement that Florida State owns the fourth quarter.

The Seminoles, after putting the final touches on another victory, will sometimes rush to midfield, raise their helmets high and perform a "group whoop," a jumping-jack victory routine that sometimes creates tension with opponents. But the tension doesn't last long. Soon everybody is joined in a group prayer—a big "amen" for a typically successful football weekend in Seminole country.

Every Saturday in Autumn · USC Trojans

THE UNIVERSITY OF
SOUTHERN CALIFORNIA

TROJANS

Tailback U., I-formations and Student Body Left. Tommy Trojan and Traveler. Seven national championships and four Heisman Trophies. John McKay, O.J. Simpson, Anthony Davis, Mike Garrett, Frank Gifford, Ricky Bell, Lynn Swann, Charles White and Marcus Allen. The Rose Bowl and the Coliseum. The Spirit of Troy band. "Conquest" and "Fight On." Notre Dame and UCLA.

Football, University of Southern California-style, is nothing if not sentimental. The images are special, the names are magic and the sounds are familiar and enduring. This is a place where tradition rolls off the tongue like defenders used to roll off the powerful body of tackle Anthony Munoz.

You don't watch football at USC, you experience it, and the tradition comes with a cardinal-and-gold flair. From Heritage Hall on the Los Angeles campus to the Memorial Coliseum on the southern edge of Exposition Park, fans can spend their football Saturdays reliving the great moments of the Trojans' colorful history, tailgating with friends, marching with the band and basking in the ambience of one of the most historic and stately sports venues ever constructed.

For engaging pageantry, for pure spectacle, there's no place like USC on game day. Football is still center stage, but, win or lose, the show will go on.

Tommy Trojan has been guarding USC's Hahn Plaza since 1930.

He stands guard over Hahn Plaza, a lone sword-wielding sentry ready to pounce on evil-minded intruders. Tall, proud and regal in his warrior attire, Tommy Trojan has served as the centerpiece of USC sports tradition for more than 70 years.

Few college landmarks can match Tommy for yeoman service—and fan appeal. Every game day, visitors flock to the center of USC's University Park campus to see the bronze statue that so elegantly represents the school's fighting spirit. On Thursday nights before homecoming and UCLA games, students party with Tommy at lively pep rallies. The Trojan has been painted blue and gold by UCLA pranksters, had his sword stolen numerous times and suffered other affronts over the years, but he perseveres with quiet dignity.

The same dignity that defines USC football, which has struggled in recent years after a glorious run during which the team won five outright or shared national titles from 1962-78 under McKay and John Robinson. The same dignity

On game day, Christmas Tree Lane becomes a sea of cardinal and gold outside the Coliseum's peristyle facade.

visitors find on a compact 155-acre campus that sits southwest of downtown Los Angeles in the Figueroa Corridor—a redevelopment area that follows Figueroa Street for about five miles from the Coliseum in Exposition Park to the downtown Staples Center.

USC, which enrolls about 29,000 students on its University Park and Health Sciences campuses, is one of the largest private research universities in the United States and a magnet for film students. Located in the shadow of Hollywood, the campus has buildings named after such luminaries as George Lucas, Steven Spielberg and Johnny Carson and it has provided location for more than 100 movies, including *The Graduate* and *The Hunchback of Notre Dame.*

That's a heady backdrop for tailgaters and picnickers, most of whom flood onto campus from their Los Angeles and Orange County homes as early as 5 a.m. for games that typically start at 12:30, 1:30 or 3:30. Many set up along Trousdale Parkway and available campus grassy areas; others blanket the historic Exposition Park grounds, home of the the country's largest rose garden, the California Science Center, the Natural History and Afro-American museums and the Los Angeles Sports Arena.

You don't watch football at USC, you experience it, and the tradition comes with a cardinal-and-gold flair.

It's a fun and festive atmosphere, spiced by the sound of fight songs, excited football chatter and pregame radio broadcasts. Adding to the aura is the Coliseum, one of the great sports arenas of the world, and the still-visible signs of two Summer Olympics that brought world-class athletes to these venerable grounds.

To capture the flavor and pageantry of Trojans football, look no further than Christmas Tree Lane—a grassy area that stretches a quarter mile or so from the Coliseum's peristyle to Figueroa

Colorful, active and prepared, the Trojan band gets avid USC fans in the proper game-day spirit.

on the eastern edge of campus. The sea of cardinal and gold will be dotted with party tents, food vendors, smoking grills and recreational vehicles with their elaborate spreads and creative menus.

It's not unusual for tailgaters near the Coliseum to get a special pregame treat—a visit from Traveler, the white Andalusian gelding with a flair for the dramatic. A real live Trojan horse.

It has been called "Hollywood's Band," "The Spirit of Troy" and "The Greatest Marching Band in the History of the Universe." By any name, the Trojan Marching Band is the soul of USC football and one of the most renowned musical groups ever assembled.

The unit, which now numbers 270, has played for 10 American presidents, appeared in five movies and numerous television shows, marched in three Super Bowls, 28 Rose Bowls and two Olympics, cut several records and appeared at numerous public celebrations, including the openings of the Disney World Epcot Center in Orlando and Disneyland Paris.

The world might be its stage, but the band is at its innovative and showy best on football weekends at USC—starting in the relative obscurity of a Friday after-noon team serenade and ending Saturday with the fun and entertaining postgame concert. Everything between is a delightful bonus.

The traditional fare begins on Friday when the band marches to the practice field and sur-rounds the team—playing, performing cheers and entertaining for about 15 minutes. This simple gesture illustrates the special bond that connects this band with the athletes it supports. The short concert ends when a senior player, preselected by the band, takes the drum major's gladiator sword, climbs the bandstand and conducts an emotional playing of "Conquest," USC's victory song.

Game day is a feverish string of early-morning rehearsals, concerts and game activity that marks USC's band as one of the most active and team-friendly units in the country. Players call the Marching Trojans inspiring; opponents offer less favorable reviews.

The real pregame show begins two hours before game time when band members, now

The Trojan and his trusty steed Traveler are a major part of USC's colorful and proud football tradition.

ing their cardinal and gold uniforms with metallic warrior helmets, gather with the USC Silks (tall flags), Song Leaders (a talented group of dancers) and Yell Leaders for the traditional march to the Coliseum. It's no coincidence that the starting point is Heritage Hall, home of the athletic offices and a museum that celebrates USC's rich football past. Inspiration is important here.

Along narrow Hellman Way, through Alumni Park and down Trousdale Parkway the band proceeds, attracting curious tailgaters and a Pied Piper-like fan following. By the time it reaches Exposition Boulevard, the "march" has become a full-fledged parade.

Tailgaters part like the Red Sea as the band winds its way past the Rose Garden and between park buildings, stopping in the Coliseum's southwest tunnel near the players' locker rooms. The first real shock for opponents comes during warmups when band members make a loud and brassy "Tunnel Run" onto the field, form a south-side line from end zone-to-end zone and provide a musical backdrop that is guaranteed to both inspire and annoy, depending on affiliation.

The cross-campus march garners even more energy on special occasions. The homecoming parade is led by the costumed Trojan aboard Traveler. And for the annual home game against hated rival UCLA or Notre Dame, the band makes a more spectacular stadium entrance down the peristyle.

It has stood, powerful and stately, for almost eight decades, a beacon for West Coast sports and a grand theater for world-impacting events. You go now to the Coliseum to enjoy the

The renovated Coliseum no longer has seating in the peristyle area, but fans watch USC games from a 2,500-seat Sun Deck behind the east end zone.

pageantry of USC football, but you leave there with so much more. The expanse, the grandeur and the architecture overwhelm you; the almost mystical sense of history inspires and affects you.

The Coliseum, the featured arena for the 1932 and '84 Olympic Games, has been the home of USC football since 1923—the same season spectacular Yankee Stadium opened a continent away. It also has provided a home for UCLA football (1929-81), the Los Angeles Rams (1946-79), the Los Angeles Chargers (1960), the Los Angeles Dodgers (1958-61) and the Los Angeles Raiders (1982-94). The only facility to host two Olympics, two Super Bowls and a World Series once attracted 134,254 people for a Billy Graham crusade.

First-time visitors are overwhelmed before they even walk in. Perched high on the main peristyle facade, a high-rising centerpiece flanked by Roman-style columns and arches, is an Olympic torch from which the flame still burns brightly. On the face of the facade are the five interlocking Olympic rings and on the outside plaza stand two headless Greek statues.

The same peristyle forms a mesmerizing backdrop for game action. The cavernous stadium, which once boasted a capacity of 101,574, now seats only 92,000 because the distant peristyle seats have been replaced by banners and oversized letters spelling out "Trojans." Although a special 2,500-seat grandstand called the "Sun Deck" has been erected behind the east end zone,

many more seats are covered by a retractable fabric, giving the Trojans a typical game-day capacity of 68,000.

But the history that drips from the Coliseum's rafters is what really floods the senses. This is where Babe Didrikson and Carl Lewis ran to Olympic glory a half century apart on a track that no longer exists. It's the same field where Garrett, Simpson, White and Allen ran to Heisman fame.

USC championship banners hang from the stadium perimeter and flags fly from the top of the south-side press box. Signs along one wall of the tunnel pay tribute to the team's 20 wins in 28 Rose Bowl appearances and the other wall encourages players to "Fight On" in large painted letters. The tradition is chilling.

The atmosphere is always upbeat and festive at USC games, even when things are not going well on the field.

So is the pageantry that opens every game. From the band's colorful fanfare and Traveler's hell-bent dash down the sideline to the team's grand entrance, it's obvious USC knows how to choreograph a show. And how to create a special atmosphere.

It begins with a flourish. After the band's pregame show, trumpets sound the recognizable first notes of "Conquest" and fans jump to their feet, flashing the traditional two-finger victory sign. Within seconds, the Trojan will burst from the tunnel aboard Traveler—the fifth in a line of white horses that have been inspiring USC players and fans since 1961.

As the crowd roars its approval, the band goes into its T-R-O-J-A-N-S formation as the warrior, brandishing his sword, rides Traveler at full gallop down the north sideline behind the USC bench. Fans barely have enough time to gasp over one of the most colorful moments in college football when the pregame focus switches dramatically to the video board perched atop the peristyle facade.

An animated flaming football swoops onto the screen, flies through Los Angeles and around the Coliseum before lighting the giant torch. As the ball moves slowly downfield, images from USC history appear on screen. When the ball reaches the tunnel, the screen goes blank before a live camera catches cheerleaders and players, decked out in eye-popping cardinal-and-gold uniforms, making their emotional burst onto the field.

Everything about USC football occurs at a frenetic pace. Unlike most bands, the Trojans play music after every down—anything from "Fight On" to special songs befitting interceptions, sacks, first downs, completions and every other play imaginable. "Tribute to Troy," the school's signature drum cadence piece, marks defensive stands and other dramatic moments. The trumpet call "Charge," a USC invention, keeps fans involved.

So do the short appearances by Traveler after every Trojans score and his dramatic run after the third quarter to the music of the William Tell Overture—a tradition that dates back to USC's dramatic 1974 comeback victory over Notre Dame. To keep the fire burning, a 10-piece band splinters from the main unit in the third quarter and parades along the walkway between levels of the stands.

Everything comes to a dramatic and lively conclusion, win or lose. After the final gun, the band forms in front of the north stands and begins playing "Conquest" as fans offer the victory salute. If the team has won, the song might be played multiple times. Finally, the Alma Mater signals a beginning for the band's special postgame concert.

For the next half hour, the band performs creative routines that will never show up in the more traditional halftime shows. Members play, dance and ad lib—punctuating their music with emphatic pelvic thrusts one minute, with lying-down, feet-wiggling verve the next—all in the spirit of the moment.

Fun and entertainment with a USC flair.

Everything, from band marches to flag running, occurs at a frenetic pace during Trojan games at the Coliseum.

SEVEN MORE TRADITIONS

Keeping Up With Ralphie

For raw power and intimidation, it's hard to top the pregame ritual that stirs up Colorado fans at Boulder's Folsom Field. Ralphie is not your typical game-day mascot. She is a 1,000-pound buffalo—a snorting, humpback bison that can run up to 25 mph in her traditional romp before football games. Accompanied by four leash-holding handlers, Ralphie leads the team out of the locker room at the start of the game and the second half and makes a mad dash around the field, much to the astonishment of wary opponents.

The current buffalo is the fourth edition of Ralphies dating back to 1966. The first buffalo (Mr. Chips) appeared in 1934, the year Colorado took its "Buffaloes" nickname.

When Ralphie runs at Folsom Field (below), the earth rumbles and everybody gets out of the way.

A Stroll Through The Grove

Down around Oxford, Miss., it's considered tailgating heaven. Thousands of game-day fans, toting their picnics and elaborate spreads, meet in The Grove—a 10-acre grassy area, shaded by large oak trees, at the center of the University of Mississippi campus.

This tailgate comes with dessert. About two hours before kickoff, everybody gathers on both sides of a walk that cuts through The Grove, greeting and shouting encouragement to Ole Miss players, who are walking to Vaught-Hemingway Stadium.

The tradition, which started in 1985 under coach Billy Brewer, continues today under David Cutcliffe. The players now walk under a "Walk of Champions" arch that was erected on the east side of The Grove in 1998—a donation from Mississippi's undefeated 1962 Rebels.

The 'Walk of Champions' arch, a portal for Mississippi players on their traditional walk to the stadium, is located on the east side of The Grove.

Ringing Endorsements

They're loud, annoying and downright distracting. And that's just fine with Mississippi State fans, who come to Scott Field armed with cowbells and a good sense of how to use them.

These aren't just ordinary cowbells. These bells come in many styles and are specially crafted for maximum loudness. They are prize possessions, weekday decorations in homes and offices, passed from generation to generation since the 1930s when, according to popular legend, a cow wandered onto the field during a victory over hated rival Mississippi, bringing State good luck.

Cowbells have been banned since 1974 at Southeastern Conference games. But they still ring outside the stadium for league games and inside against nonconference opponents. More daring fans still risk confiscation of their prize bells in important games against SEC foes.

All Aboard for South Carolina

It's appropriately named the Cockaboose Railroad, a string of 22 cabooses that line an isolated stretch of track on the south side of South Carolina's Williams-Brice Stadium. This is a special kind of railroad, a stationary "train" on which Gamecock passengers participate in a unique tailgating tradition.

All 22 of the "cabooses" were specially constructed and elegantly equipped with the high-powered alumni in mind. Each interior is designed with a special motif, and each caboose offers all the comforts of home—living-room areas, bars, running water, cable television, air conditioning, heating and even sleeping quarters. Tailgaters often entertain and grill on top of the cars, creating a patio-like atmosphere.

The Cockaboose Railroad was created in 1990, the brainstorm of Columbia businessman Ed Robinson. Each caboose is individually owned.

In a Pig's Eye

He's fat, pig-headed and something of a boar. But don't make fun of Tusk I in front of Arkansas fans, who view their live mascot with deep-rooted affection.

Tusk I, a Russian boar, is about as close as you can get to a true Razorback. He has attended in-state Arkansas games since 1997, when he replaced the last of 10 "Big Reds" that had served as team mascots since the 1960s.

But nothing says Arkansas football more than the arm-raising "Wooo, Pig! Sooie!" cheer, which is performed over and over with enthusiastic pride on game day at Fayetteville. The so-called "Battle Cry of the Ozarks" was first heard in the 1920s, a heartfelt gift from local farmers.

Heartfelt as in goosebumps. Razorbacks coach Houston Nutt says he still gets them every time he hears the "Sooie" cry, just like he did when he was a player at Arkansas.

Scattering at Stanford

If you don't believe that the Stanford Band marches to a different drummer, just watch it on game day. Precision marches, perfectly choreographed programs, pomp and circumstance—those things are for the more traditional bands at almost every other university.

Stanford's "scatter" band, a student-run unit that tests the patience of university officials, is more about humor, irreverence and poking fun, which is not always well received. The band got into hot water one year when it made fun of the Pope and the Irish potato famine in a game against Notre Dame. UCLA players, who had come under fire for parking in handicapped spots, were the target another time when the band formed a human handicapped-parking sign and Oregon fans cringed at a routine that made fun of spotted owls.

Stanford's band mascot, a silly-acting tree, changes size and look annually.

Funny ties, floppy hats and witty buttons adorn basic uniforms that are anything but traditional. And the band is accompanied by a silly-acting Tree mascot that changes shape and style every year. Why a tree? Only Stanford's "anti-band" knows for sure.

Navy Seal of Approval

Every pregame show at the U.S. Naval Academy in Annapolis is a spine-tingling experience, starting with a patriotic march of the entire brigade of Midshipmen into Navy-Marine Corps Memorial Stadium. This salute to school, team and country is well worth the price of admission, but it's only a prelude to the real show.

After the national anthem, sung by current Midshipmen, all eyes look skyward as F-18 fighter jets buzz the stadium, offering their own special and dramatic fan welcome. Then 12 members of the Navy Seal Leap Frog Parachute Team punctuate the show with a 30,000-foot jump during which they perform acrobatic stunts before landing on the field below.